GOSPEL SHAPED

WORSHIP

Leader's Guide

GOSPEL SHAPED
WORSHIP

Jared C. Wilson

 THE GOSPEL COALITION    thegoodbook COMPANY

Gospel Shaped Worship Leader's Guide
© The Gospel Coalition / The Good Book Company 2015

Published by:
The Good Book Company
Tel (US): 866 244 2165
Tel (UK): 0333 123 0880
Email (US): info@thegoodbook.com
Email (UK): info@thegoodbook.co.uk

Websites:
North America: www.thegoodbook.com
UK: www.thegoodbook.co.uk
Australia: www.thegoodbook.com.au
New Zealand: www.thegoodbook.co.nz

ISBN: 9781909919204 Printed in the US

PRODUCTION TEAM:

AUTHOR:
Jared C. Wilson

**SERIES EDITOR FOR
THE GOSPEL COALITION:**
Collin Hansen

**SERIES EDITOR FOR
THE GOOD BOOK COMPANY:**
Tim Thornborough

**MAIN TEACHING SESSION
DISCUSSIONS:** Alison Mitchell

DAILY DEVOTIONALS:
Carl Laferton

BIBLE STUDIES:
Tim Thornborough

EDITORIAL ASSISTANTS:
Jeff Robinson (TGC), Rachel Jones (TGBC)

VIDEO EDITOR:
Phil Grout

PROJECT ADMINISTRATOR:
Jackie Moralee

EXECUTIVE PRODUCER:
Brad Byrd

DESIGN:
André Parker

 CONTENTS

 **PREFACE**

GROWING A GOSPEL SHAPED CHURCH

The Gospel Coalition is a group of pastors and churches in the Reformed heritage who delight in the truth and power of the gospel, and who want the gospel of Christ crucified and resurrected to lie at the center of all we cherish, preach and teach.

We want churches called into existence by the gospel to be shaped by the gospel in their everyday life.

Through our fellowship, conferences, and online and printed media, we have sought to encourage pastors and church leaders to calibrate their lives around what is of first importance—the gospel of Christ. In these resources, we want to provide those same pastors with the tools to excite and equip church members with this mindset.

In our foundation documents, we identified five areas that should mark the lives of believers in a local fellowship:

1. Empowered corporate worship
2. Evangelistic effectiveness
3. Counter-cultural community
4. The integration of faith and work
5. The doing of justice and mercy

We believe that a church utterly committed to winsome and theologically substantial expository preaching, and that lives out the gospel in these areas, will display its commitment to dynamic evangelism, apologetics, and church planting. These gospel-shaped churches will emphasize repentance, personal renewal, holiness, and the wonderful life of the church as the body of Christ. At the same time, there will be engagement with the social structures of ordinary people, and cultural engagement with art, business, scholarship and government. The church will be characterized by firm devotion to the truth on the one hand, and by transparent compassion on the other.

The Gospel Coalition believes in the priority of the local church, and that the local church is the best place to discuss these five ministry drivers and decide how to integrate them into life and mission. So, while being clear on the biblical principles, these resources give space to consider what a genuine expression of a gospel-shaped church looks like for you in the place where God has put you, and with the people he has gathered into fellowship with you.

Through formal teaching sessions, daily Bible devotionals, group Bible studies and the regular preaching ministry, it is our hope and prayer that congregations will grow into maturity, and so honor and glorify our great God and Savior.

Don Carson
President

Tim Keller
Vice President

INTRODUCTION

I think you could make a pretty good case that evangelicals don't really know what worship is—or, at least, they don't really know what worship *fully* is.

Scroll through your social media feeds on a typical Sunday morning and you will see lots of talk among your churchgoing friends about worship—but I'd be willing to bet that most of that talk is focused entirely on *music*.

But worship is more than a genre of music or one section of a worship service. Even to speak of worship largely in terms of a worship service is not to do the subject justice. We tend to talk in compartmentalized ways about something that by its very nature cannot be compartmentalized; because, according to the Bible, worship is *every human being's way of life*. We are never not worshiping. We just can't help it.

At each and every moment of our lives, we are living in a way that "gives worth" to something. For many people, their ideas of worth are centered on themselves, or their family or their job. In one way or another we are worshiping ourselves. But for those who have discovered the grace of God in Jesus Christ, a massive change has taken place. By the power of the Holy Spirit in our lives, we are enabled to start worshiping the one true God instead of the many false gods we fill our lives with.

What is true for us as individuals is true for us as a gathered community of God's people. We discover in the Bible that a church that is centered on the gospel of Jesus Christ will be shaped by the gospel of Jesus Christ. And a church shaped by the gospel of Jesus Christ will see that its true "service of worship" is conducted both inside the formal gathering of believers and outside it as well.

We worship when we sing, yes, but we also worship when we preach and receive preaching, when we pray, when we share the gospel, and when we love our neighbors in a million different ways throughout the week.

The Gospel Coalition has included this statement in their Theological Vision for Ministry, entitled "Empowered corporate worship":

The gospel changes our relationship with God from one of hostility or slavish compliance to one of intimacy and joy. The core dynamic of gospel-centered ministry is therefore worship and fervent prayer.

In corporate worship God's people receive a special life-transforming sight of the worth and beauty of God, and then give back to God suitable expressions of his worth. At the heart of corporate worship is the ministry of the Word.

In each session, our aim is to refresh our sense of God's love for us in Christ, so that every aspect of our community life would be shaped by the gospel and lead us to glorify the God who supplies his grace so abundantly in Jesus.

And as you work through this program as a church together, my hope is that you will capture a vision of worship that goes way beyond a song or a service on Sunday morning. I pray that you will discover an enlarged and empowered vision for your life as a worshiper, as we look again and again into Christ's glory in the gospel found in his word.

Jared C. Wilson

MAKING THE MOST OF
GOSPEL SHAPED
CHURCH

WHAT GOSPEL SHAPED CHURCH WILL DO FOR YOU

God is in the business of changing people and changing churches. He always does that through his gospel.

Through the gospel he changed us from his enemies to his friends, and through the gospel he brought us into a new family to care for each other and to do his will in the world. The gospel brings life and creates churches.

But the gospel of Jesus, God's Son, our Savior and Lord, isn't merely what begins our Christian life and forms new churches. It is the pattern, and provides the impetus, for all that follows. So Paul wrote to the Colossian church:

> *Therefore, as you received Christ Jesus the Lord, so walk in him, rooted and built up in him and established in the faith, just as you were taught, abounding in thanksgiving (Colossians 2:6-7).*

Just as you received … so walk… In other words, the secret of growing as a Christian is to continue to reflect upon and build your life on the gospel of the lordship of Jesus Christ. And the secret of growing as a church is to let the gospel inform and energize every single aspect of a church's life, both in what you do and how you do it, from your sermons to young mothers' groups; from your budget decisions and your pastoral care to your buildings maintenance and church bulletins.

Letting the gospel shape a church requires the whole church to be shaped by the gospel. To be, and become, gospel shaped is not a task merely for the senior pastor, or the staff team, or the board of elders. It is something that happens as every member considers the way in which the gospel should continue to shape their walk, and the life of their church.

That is the conviction that lies behind this series of five resources from The Gospel Coalition. It will invite your church members to be part of the way in which you shape your church according to the unchanging gospel, in your particular culture and circumstances. It will excite and equip your whole church to be gospel shaped. It will envision you together, from senior church staff to your newest believer. It will enable you all to own the vision of a gospel-shaped church, striving to teach that gospel to one another and to reach your community with that gospel. As you continue to work out together the implications of the gospel that has saved us, you will be guided into Christian maturity in every area of your lives, both personal and corporate.

This resource is for all kinds of churches: large and small; urban and rural; new plants and long-established congregations; all denominations and none. It is for any congregation that has been given life by the gospel and wants to put the gospel at the center of its life.

You can use the five tracks in any order you like—and you can use as many or as few of them as you wish. If you think your church is lacking in one particular area, it will always be helpful to focus on that for a season. But it is our hope that you will plan to run all five parts of the curriculum with your church—perhaps over a 3- or 4-year time frame. Some tracks may be more like revision and confirmation that you are working well in those areas. Others will open up new areas of service and change that you need to reflect upon. But together they will help you grow into an organic maturity as you reflect on the implications of the gospel in every area of life.

HOW TO MAKE THE MOST OF THIS CURRICULUM

Because the gospel, as it is articulated in the pages of the Bible, should be the foundation of everything we do, this resource is designed to work best if a congregation gives itself over to exploring the themes together as a whole. That means shaping the whole of church life for a season around the theme. The overall aim is to get the DNA of the gospel into the DNA of your church life, structures, practices and people.

So it is vitally important that you involve as many people in your congregation as possible in the process, so that there is a sense that this is a journey that the whole church has embarked upon together. The more you immerse yourselves in this material, the more you will get from it. But equally, all churches are different, and so this material is flexible enough to fit any and every church program and structure—see page 24 for more details.

Here are some other suggestions for how to make the most of this material.

PREPARE

Work through the material in outline with your leadership team and decide which elements best fit where. Will you use the sermon suggestions, or develop a series of your own? Will you teach through the main sessions in Sunday School, or in midweek groups? Will you use the teaching DVD, or give your own talks?

Think about some of the likely pressure points this discussion will create in your congregation. How will you handle in a constructive way any differences of opinion that come out of this? Decide together how you will handle feedback. There will be many opportunities for congregation members to express their ideas and thoughts, and as you invite them to think about your church's life, they will have many suggestions. It will be overwhelming to have everyone emailing or calling the Senior Pastor; but it will be very frustrating if church members feel they are not truly being listened to, and that nothing will really change. So organize a system of feedback from group-discussion leaders and Bible-study leaders; make clear which member of senior staff will collect that feedback; and schedule time as a staff team to listen to your members' thoughts, and pray about and consider them.

There is an online feedback form that could be distributed and used to round off the whole track with your congregation.

PROMOTE

Encourage your congregation to buy into the process by promoting it regularly and building anticipation. Show the trailer at all your church meetings and distribute your own customized version of the bulletin insert (download from www.gospelshapedchurch.org).

Embarking on this course together should be a big deal. Make sure your congregation knows what it might mean for them, and what an opportunity it represents in the life of your whole church; and make sure it sounds like an exciting adventure in faith.

Do involve the whole church. Younger children may not be able to grasp the implications of some things, but certainly those who teach and encourage children of 11 and upwards will be able to adapt the material and outlines here to something that is age appropriate.

PRAY

Pray as a leadership team that the Lord would lead you all into new, exciting ways of serving him.

Encourage the congregation to pray. There are plenty of prompts in the material for this to happen, but do pray at your regular meetings for the Lord's help and guidance as you study, think and discuss together. Building in regular prayer times will help your congregation move together as a fellowship. Prayer connects us to God, but it also connects us to each other, as we address our Father together. And our God "is able to do far more abundantly than all that we ask or think" (Ephesians 3:20-21) as his people ask him to enable them to grasp, and be shaped by, the love of Christ that is shown to us in his gospel.

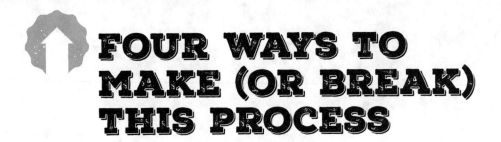

FOUR WAYS TO MAKE (OR BREAK) THIS PROCESS

1. BE OPEN TO CHANGE AS A CHURCH

As churches that love the gospel, we should always be reforming to live more and more in line with that gospel. Change isn't always easy, and is often sacrificial; but it is exciting, and part of the way in which we obey our Lord. Approach this exploration of **Gospel Shaped Worship** by encouraging your church to be willing to change where needed.

2. BE OPEN TO CHANGE YOURSELF

This curriculum will lead every member to think hard about how the gospel should shape, and in some ways re-shape, your church. You are giving them permission to suggest making changes. As a leader, giving such permission is both exciting and intimidating. It will *make* your course if you enter it as a leadership excited to see how your church may change and how you may be challenged. It will *break* it if you approach it hoping or expecting that your members will simply agree in every way with what you have already decided.

3. DISCUSS GRACIOUSLY

Keep talking about grace and community. Church is about serving others and giving up "my" own wants, not about meeting "my" own social preferences and musical tastes. Encourage your membership to pursue discussions that are positive, open and non-judgmental, and to be able to disagree lovingly and consider other's feelings before their own, rather than seeking always to "win." Model gospel grace in the way you talk about the gospel of grace.

4. REMEMBER WHO IS IN CHARGE

Jesus Christ is Lord of your church—not the leadership, the elders or the membership. So this whole process needs to be bathed in a prayerful sense of commitment to follow him, and to depend on his strength and guidance for any change his Spirit is prompting. Keep reminding your church that this process is not about becoming the church they want, but the one your Lord wants.

HOW TO USE

GOSPEL SHAPED
WORSHIP

HOW TO USE GOSPEL SHAPED WORSHIP

Gospel Shaped Worship is designed to be a flexible resource to fit a wide variety of church settings. The **Main Teaching Session** is the core of the curriculum—the other components grow out of this. The more elements you use, the greater the benefit will be to your church.

The elements of this course are:

- **MAIN TEACHING SESSION** with DVD or talk, and discussion (core)
- **PERSONAL DEVOTIONALS** (recommended)
- **GROUP BIBLE STUDY** (recommended)
- **PERSONAL JOURNAL** (optional)
- **SERMON SERIES** (suggested passages given)

Each church member will need a copy of the *Gospel Shaped Worship Handbook*. This contains everything they need to take part in the course, including the discussion questions for the **Main Teaching Session**, **Personal Devotionals**, and the **Group Bible Study**. There's also space to make notes during the sermon, and a **Personal Journal** to keep a record of the things they have been learning.

Each person who will be leading a group discussion, either in the **Main Teaching Session** or the **Group Bible Study**, will need a copy of the *Gospel Shaped Worship Leader's Guide*. This includes leader's notes to help them guide a small group through the discussion or Bible-study questions, and other resources to give more background and detail. In the Leader's Guide, all the instructions, questions, comments, prayer points etc. that also appear in the Handbook are in **bold text**.

 Further copies of the *Handbook* and *Leader's Guide* are available from **WWW.GOSPELSHAPEDCHURCH.ORG/WORSHIP**

A FLEXIBLE CURRICULUM

Gospel Shaped Worship is designed to be a flexible resource. You may be able to give your whole church over to working through it. If so, a typical week might look like this:

SUNDAY
- Adult Sunday school: **Main Teaching Session** using DVD or live talk (talk outline given in *Leader's Guide*)
- Morning service: **Sermon** based on main theme (suggested Bible passages given in the *Leader's Guide*)

MIDWEEK
- Small groups work through the **Group Bible Study**

CHURCH MEMBERS
- Use the **Personal Devotionals** from Monday to Saturday
- Use the **Personal Journal** to record their thoughts, questions and ideas about things they've been learning throughout the week

Or, if you choose to use the curriculum on a midweek basis, it may be like this:

MIDWEEK
- Small groups work through the **Main Teaching Session** using the DVD

CHURCH MEMBERS
- Use the **Personal Devotionals** from Monday to Saturday
- Use the **Personal Journal** to record their thoughts, questions and ideas about things they've been learning throughout the week

Or you can use the components in any other way that suits your church practice.

HOW TO USE EACH ELEMENT

These sample pages from the *Gospel Shaped Worship Handbook* show the different elements of the curriculum.

All of the material in this curriculum quotes from and is based on the ESV Bible.

MAIN TEACHING SESSION

- 60 minutes
- Choose between DVD or live talk
- Discussion questions to help group members discuss the DVD/talk and apply it to their own lives and their church
- Guidance for answering the questions is given in the *Leader's Guide*
- Suggestions for praying together

This is the core of the curriculum. It can be run using the *Gospel Shaped Worship DVD*, or by giving a live talk. A summary of the talk is included in the *Leader's Guide* (see page 34 for an example). A full editable script can also be downloaded from **www.gospelshapedchurch.org/worship/talks**.

In each session, the DVD/talk is split into either two or three sections, each followed by some discussion questions. At the end of the session there are suggestions to help the group pray specifically for each other.

The discussion questions are designed to help church members unpack the teaching they have heard and apply it to their own lives and to the church as a whole. There are not necessarily right and wrong answers to some of the questions, as this will often depend on the context of your own church. Let group members discuss these openly, and apply them to their own situation.

Keep the discussion groups the same each week if possible, with the same leader (who will need a copy of this *Leader's Guide*) for each group, so that relationships are deepened and the discussions can build on those of previous sessions.

PERSONAL DEVOTIONALS

- Six devotionals with each session
- Designed to be started the day after the main teaching session
- Linked with the theme for each teaching session, but based on different Bible passages
- Help church members dig more deeply into the theme on a daily basis

Each session is followed by six personal devotionals that build on the main theme. They are ideal for church members to use between sessions. For example, if you have the main teaching session on a Sunday, church members can then use the devotionals from Monday to Saturday.

These short devotionals can be used in addition to any regular personal Bible study being done by church members. They would also form a useful introduction for anyone trying out personal Bible reading for the first time.

As well as being in the group member's *Handbook*, the personal devotionals are available for a small fee on the Explore Bible Devotional app. This can be downloaded from the iTunes App Store or Google Play (search for "Explore Bible Devotional"). Select "Gospel Shaped Worship" from the app's download menu.

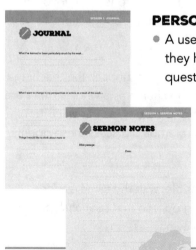

PERSONAL JOURNAL

- A useful place for church members to note down what they have been learning throughout the week, and any questions they may have.

SERMON NOTES

- If the Sunday sermon series is running as part of *Gospel Shaped Worship*, this is a helpful place to make notes.

GROUP BIBLE STUDY

- 40 – 50 minutes
- An ideal way for small groups to build on what they have been learning in the main teaching
- Uses a different Bible passage from the DVD/talk
- Suggested answers to the questions are given in the *Leader's Guide*

This study is ideal for a home group or other group to work through together. It builds on the theme covered by the main teaching session, but is based on a different Bible passage. You can see the passages and themes listed in the grid on pages 28-29.

If possible, give 40 – 50 minutes for the Bible study. However, it can be covered in 30 minutes if necessary, and if you keep a close eye on time. If your church is not using the Bible studies as part of a regular group, they would also be suitable for individuals to do on their own or in a pair if they want to do some further study on the themes being looked at in the course. The Bible study in session 2 (on pages 59-63) would also be ideal for a leader to use one on one with any group members who may not be clear on the core gospel message.

SERMON SUGGESTIONS

The *Leader's Guide* gives a choice of three sermon suggestions to tie in with each session:

- A passage that is used in the main teaching session (DVD or live talk).
- The Bible reading that is being studied in the Group Bible Study that week.
- A third passage that is not being used elsewhere, but that picks up on the same themes. This is the passage that is listed in the overview grid on pages 28-29.

FURTHER READING

At the end of each session in the *Leader's Guide* you will find a page of suggestions for further reading. This gives ideas for books, articles, blog posts, videos, etc. that relate to the session, together with some quotes that you might use in sermons, discussion groups and conversations. Some of these may be helpful in your preparation, as well as helping any group members who want to think more deeply about the topic they've been discussing.

CURRICULUM OUTLINE AT A GLANCE

SESSION	MAIN TEACHING (DVD/TALK)	PERSONAL DEVOTIONS	GROUP BIBLE STUDY	SERMON*
1 What is worship?	What is worship and why do we worship God? Based on **Mark 12:28-31** and **Luke 6:45**.	**Romans 12:1-8**, looking at what motivates our worship, what our worship is and what it results in.	**Psalm 16** God is of supreme worth. What is the experience of being a true worshiper like?	PSALM 96
2 The foundation of worship	God's grace toward us in Christ is the foundation of true worship. Various passages including **1 Corinthians 15: 1-4** and **Romans 1:16**.	Looking at how Old Testament history shows us our need for a Savior-King, and how God promises his people just that. **Genesis; Exodus; Numbers; 2 Samuel; Hosea** and **Matthew**.	**Titus 3:3-8** Reinforcing the key message of the gospel. *(This study can also be used one on one with any group members who are not entirely clear about the gospel message.)*	MARK 1:14-15
3 Worship and God's word	Worship is a response to God's gospel call through the whole Bible. Various passages including **1 Corinthians 15:3; Romans 10:13-15; Nehemiah 8:9-12** and **2 Timothy 3:16-17**.	Six New Testament passages in which God calls us to respond to the gospel of Jesus Christ in different ways. **Luke; Romans; James; 1 Peter; Philippians** and **Ephesians**.	**2 Timothy 3:14 – 4:8** The centrality of the word of God to our lives as believers, and its central place in our gatherings.	PSALM 119:169-176
4 The worship service	The worship service is for gathering the church, worshiping the Lord, remembering the gospel, shaping the church and sending on mission. Various passages including **Acts 2:41-47**.	A detailed look from various passages at the elements of the worship service mentioned in **Acts 2:42-47**: teaching, fellowship, breaking bread, prayer, giving and praise.	**Hebrews 10:19-31** Reinforcing how the gospel should be the heart and shape of our gathered worship.	1 COR 11:17-34

	SESSION	MAIN TEACHING (DVD/TALK)	PERSONAL DEVOTIONS	GROUP BIBLE STUDY	SERMON*
5	Why and how we pray	Our prayers should be shaped by the gospel. Based on **Matthew 6:9-13** and **John 17:18-21**.	The story of Hannah in **1 Samuel 1:1 – 2:11** as she shows us when, how and why we are to pray.	**Colossians 1:9-14** What does gospel-shaped prayer look like in practice?	EPH 3:14-21
6	Developing a culture of grace	The gospel, rightly understood and applied, turns us into a community of grace toward each other and to all people. Based on **Romans 15:1-7**.	**Revelation 1, 2, 3 and 7**, moving from a vision of the risen Jesus to a vision of the heavenly throne room, via the Lord's letters to seven churches, and to ours.	**Colossians 3:5-14** How does gospel-shaped worship feed into a culture of practical grace?	1 COR 12:12-31
7	Being church	We worship by committing to love one another and the world. Based on **Romans 12:9-21**.	These studies in **Ephesians 4 – 6** show us many ways to worship: as church, in our personal holiness, at home and at work.	**Romans 12:1-2, 9-21** We worship Jesus as we live grace-filled lives that are on show to outsiders through our day-to-day interactions as the church family— and as we show practical compassion to the world.	1 COR 13:1-13

* **NOTE:** The *Leader's Guide* gives three sermon suggestions to tie in with each session. The first picks up a passage from the Main Teaching Session; the second uses the passage from the Group Bible Study; and the third is a new passage, linked with the theme but not used elsewhere in the session. This third passage is the one listed here.

DOWNLOADS

In addition to the material in this **Leader's Guide**, there are a number of extra downloadable resources and enhancements. You will find all of them listed under the Worship track at **www.gospelshapedchurch.org** and on The Good Book Company's website: **www.thegoodbook.com/gsc**.

- **DIGITAL DOWNLOAD OF DVD MATERIAL.** If you have already bought a DVD as part of the **Leader's Kit**, you will have access to a single HD download of the material using the code on the download card. If you want to download additional digital copies, in SD or HD, these can be purchased from The Good Book Company website: **www.thegoodbook.com/gsc**.

- **DVD TRAILERS.** Trailers and promotional pieces for the series as a whole and for the individual tracks can be downloaded for free. Use these trailers to excite your church about being involved in **Gospel Shaped Church**.

- **TALK TRANSCRIPTS.** We're conscious that for some churches and situations, it may be better to deliver your own talk for the main session so that it can be tailored specifically to your people and context. You can download the talk transcript as both a PDF and as an editable Word document.

- **FEEDBACK FORMS.** Because **Gospel Shaped Church** is designed as a whole-church exploration, it's important that you think through carefully how you will handle suggestions and feedback. There's some guidance for that on pages 17-18. We've provided a downloadable feedback form that you can use as part of the way in which you end your time using the resource. Simply print it and distribute it to your church membership to gather their thoughts and ideas, and to get a sense of the issues you may want to focus on for the future. In addition, there are also fully editable versions of this feedback form so that you can create your own customized sheet that works effectively for the way in which you have used this material, and which suits your church membership. Alternatively, you could use the questions to create your own online feedback form with Google Forms or some other software, to make collecting and collating information easier.

- **RESOURCE LIST.** For each session in this *Leader's Guide* we have included a list of resources that will help you in your preparation for sermons, discussions, Bible studies and other conversations. On the *Gospel Shaped Church* website, you will find an up-to-date list of resources, plus a shorter downloadable list that you might consider giving to church members to supplement their own reading and thinking.

- **BULLETIN TEMPLATES.** Enclosed with the *Leader's Kit* is a sample of a bulletin-insert design to promote the Worship track to your church. You can download a printable PDF of the design from the *Gospel Shaped Church* website to add your own details, and to print and distribute to your congregation.

- **OTHER PROMOTIONAL MATERIAL.** Editable powerpoint slides and other promotional material to use.

 WWW.GOSPELSHAPEDCHURCH.ORG/WORSHIP

 WWW.THEGOODBOOK.COM/GSC/WORSHIP

SESSION 1:

WHAT IS WORSHIP?

"WORSHIP" IS ONE OF THE WORDS MOST COMMONLY USED IN CHURCHES AND BY CHRISTIANS. BUT WHAT DOES IT ACTUALLY MEAN? WHAT IS IT, AND WHEN DO WE DO IT? THESE ARE THE QUESTIONS WE CONSIDER IN THIS FIRST SESSION; AND, AS WE'LL SEE, THE ANSWERS ARE EXCITING AND ALL-ENCOMPASSING.

TALK OUTLINE

1.1 ● What is worship? A church service? Singing on a Sunday morning?
Worship is a whole way of living; it's how we express who or what we find valuable. To worship something is to give worth to that thing.

● **WE ARE ALWAYS WORSHIPING** *Mark 12:28-31*
  - Jesus is not talking about a list of things to do, but a whole way of being: all-encompassing love.
  - We are always worshiping someone or something. We love what we worship; so to love God with all we have is to worship him alone.
  - When we worship anything other than God, it is idolatry.

1.2 ● **ACCEPTABLE WORSHIP**
  - It's easy to fall into socially acceptable idolatry: worshiping the gifts instead of the Giver. This can happen on an individual and a whole-church level. (Give examples from your own culture and church.)
  - We are to love God with our mind and our affections. Worship should identify the only worthy object of worship (God) and truths *about* him.

● **SPIRITUAL WORSHIP** *Luke 6:45; Mark 12:29*
  - Belief drives behavior. Acceptable worship flows from an acceptable heart.
  - Mark 12:29 looks back to who God is. As Christians, we look back to the cross. Worship is to be the outflow of a heart that is believing in the gospel, as revealed by the Spirit.

● **WORSHIP ON MISSION** *Mark 12:31*
  - The commands to love God and to love others are inextricably connected.
  - Spirit-empowered, whole-life worship becomes a means of witness.
  - We are on mission to proclaim Christ where he is not worshiped.

● **CONCLUSION:** Let's start using the word "worship" correctly. It's about knowing and sharing God's love in our lives at every moment of every day.

You can download a full transcript of these talks at
WWW.GOSPELSHAPEDCHURCH.ORG/WORSHIP/TALKS

WHAT IS WORSHIP?

* Ask the group members to turn to Session 1 on page 13 of the Handbook.

Discuss

What comes into your mind when you hear the word "worship"?

This starter question is to get people thinking and talking about the concept of worship. Depending on the make-up of your group, there may be a range of ideas and experiences that come into people's minds. There is no wrong answer to this question—the aim is just to get people talking.

▶ **WATCH DVD 1.1** (8 min 23 sec) **OR DELIVER TALK 1.1** (see page 34)

* Encourage the group to make notes as they watch the DVD or listen to the talk. There is space for notes on page 15 of the Handbook.

"Worship means to give worth or value to something. It expresses what we find most valuable or satisfying." How is this a wider definition of worship than we often use?

In the opening question, group members may have associated worship mainly with singing and/or elements of a Sunday "worship service." The same was true in the *Marty and Susan* clip on the DVD. These are valid examples of worship: when we sing praises to God, we are declaring his worth; when we use liturgy together, we are reminding each other of his true value; when we are taught from Scripture, we recognize the authority of God's word in our lives. All of these are aspects of worship.

But encourage your group to think more widely than this. A biblical understanding of worship impacts every part of our lives and beings as we ask who or what we give the most worth or value to.

 **MARK 12:28-31**

> *28 And one of the scribes came up and heard them disputing with one another, and seeing that he answered them well, asked him, "Which commandment is the most important of all?" 29 Jesus answered, "The most important is, 'Hear, O Israel: The Lord our God, the Lord is one. 30 And you shall love the Lord your God with all your heart and with all your soul and with all your mind and with all your strength.' 31 The second is this: 'You shall love your neighbor as yourself.' There is no other commandment greater than these."*

God is of far greater worth than anyone or anything else. How do we show that we understand this, according to Jesus?

We show our understanding of God's worth by obeying his command to love him in every way possible. This kind of love isn't just a feeling—it impacts who we are and what we do (heart, soul, mind and strength).

Would you consider Jesus' answer a description of worship? Why or why not?

The question will help to unpack what the group understands about worship. If they still think that worship is mainly about singing, then this will seem to match part of Jesus' command, but not all of it. However, if we think of worship as "giving worth" to something, we can see a much closer link to the command to love God in every way. Since God is of far greater worth than anyone or anything else, a right response is to love him more than anyone or anything else.

NOTE: These commands did not originate with Jesus—they come from the Old Testament (Deuteronomy 6:4-5; Leviticus 19:18). Loving God fully in this way has *always* been the right response to who he is.

In the DVD, Jared asked the following questions:
- *What animates you most, energizes you most, captivates you most, stirs and inspires and motivates you most?*
- *What, based on your daily life and behavior, would people say is the most important thing to you?*

How would someone who knew you well answer these questions?

Encourage the group to give honest answers to these questions. As they imagine what their lives look like to someone else, it will help them to see what they really "give worth to" (with their time, money, attention, etc.), rather than what they think or hope they give worth to. Be ready to give an example of your own, if needed, to start the conversation.

How might an outside observer answer them about your church, based on: a) your Sunday services? b) seeing what you are like outside of formal services?

a) Think about a typical Sunday meeting (which may possibly be called a "worship service"). If a non-Christian visitor joined you for a service, what would they see you giving the most focus and energy to? What would they think inspires you? What would you be giving the most "worth" to?

b) Think of ways and places in which an outside observer could see some/ all of the church family together other than during a Sunday service. This might include mingling together before and after a service, sharing Sunday lunch together, meeting mid-week, doing things together in or for the local community, etc. What would you be talking about? What would you be excited about? What would you be giving most "worth" to?

▶ **WATCH DVD 1.2** (6 min 50 sec) **OR DELIVER TALK 1.2** (see page 34)

* Encourage the group to make notes as they watch the DVD or listen to the talk. There is space for notes on page 17 of the Handbook.

Discuss

What might be some examples of socially acceptable idolatry within evangelical churches?

Think in terms of both individuals and whole churches. In both cases, the danger is taking something good that God has given us and beginning to focus on that thing, rather than the God who gives it—we turn a "good thing" into a "God thing." For individuals, this might include such things as marriage, children (particularly education), comfort, church involvement, good works, career or educational success. For a church, it could be pride in the size of our congregation, our building, our pastor, our great music group, or having "better teaching" than the church down the road.

Why is this kind of idolatry more difficult for us to see?

It's more difficult to see because the thing or person we are giving worth to is a "good" thing. If we're addicted to pornography, it's easy to see this as idolatry because we know that using porn is a sin, and we are treating it as more important than obeying God. However, it's harder to spot if we put too much value on our marriage or children, because these are good things (unless we allow them to become more important to us than the God who has given them to us).

LUKE 6:45

[Jesus said:] *"The good person out of the good treasure of his heart produces good, and the evil person out of his evil treasure produces evil, for out of the abundance of the heart his mouth speaks."*

"Jesus is saying that acceptable worship comes from an acceptable heart." **Why is this both a liberating and a challenging truth for us?**

It is *liberating* because it isn't based on our abilities or knowledge or experience as a Christian. We aren't limited by lack of ability to sing God's praises beautifully, quote long sections of Scripture or pray eloquently. An acceptable heart is one that knows and trusts Jesus, and this is a change that is worked within us by the Holy Spirit—it is not dependent on anything we do.

At the same time, this truth is *challenging* because we have seen how easily our hearts become focused on someone or something other than God. We need to ask him to forgive us when we fall into idolatry, and to work in our lives so that we will be able to love him with all our heart, soul, mind and strength.

Summary

How would you now define the word "worship"?

Ask group members to write their answers in their Handbook, using their own words. Then ask a few to share what they have written. This will be an opportunity to discover whether some of the group are still struggling to understand what biblical worship is. If needed, it may be helpful to refer them back to the definition on page 15 of the Handbook, where it says that: *"Worship means to give worth or value to something. It expresses what we find most valuable or satisfying."* Then ask the group to explain this in their own words.

Do you find yourself or your church using the word "worship" in an unhelpfully restrictive way? What consequences does/might this have?

- If we restrict worship to singing God's praises, we will put too much focus on the music.
- If we believe a church only worships together at a Sunday gathering, we will avoid thinking of other ways in which we can worship together as a church family.
- If we think that worship is something we only do when meeting with others in a "religious" context, we won't challenge ourselves as to how we can love God with all our heart, soul, mind and strength day by day.

"Let's start using the word 'worship' in the right way. Not just about gathering and singing together, but about knowing and sharing the love of God in our lives at every moment of every day."

Think of two ways in which you will "worship God" differently this week. Ask the rest of your group to pray for you as you do this.

Encourage your group each to think of two ways and write them in their Handbooks. You may want to pair up group members so that they pray for each other and hold each other accountable (eg: asking regularly how things are going, and encouraging their partner to worship God in every aspect of their lives).

Pray

Pray that as you all work through this curriculum, you will grow in your understanding of who God is and all he has done for you, and that you will reflect this as a church family.

Pray that you will have acceptable hearts that lead you to worship God. Pray that your love for God will also produce love for your neighbors.

DAILY BIBLE DEVOTIONALS

As you finish the session, point group members to the daily devotionals to do at home over the course of the next week. There are six of them, beginning on page 21, and followed by a page for journaling. This week the devotionals walk through Romans 12:1-8, where Paul shows what motivates our worship (the gospel), what our worship is (whole-life, sacrificial obedience), and what our worship results in (a life that is pleasing to God).

SERMONS

 OPTION ONE: MARK 12:28-34

Jared focuses on part of this passage in his DVD presentation, and you could expand upon it in a longer sermon.

OPTION TWO: PSALM 16

This is the passage the Bible study is based on (see next page), which could also be expanded upon in a sermon.

 OPTION THREE: PSALM 96

This passage is not mentioned in this material, but picks up on several of the themes of this session, especially the following:
- We are commanded to sing praise to the Lord (v 1-2).
- We are commanded to call others to worship him too, telling them of his glory, salvation, rule and judgment (v 1-3, 10).
- We do this in response to who God is (v 4-9).

If one of your Sunday sermons is to be based on the theme of this session, church members will find a page to write notes on the sermon on page 31 of their Handbooks.

BIBLE STUDY

AIM: The main teaching session this week looked at why we worship God—because he is what is most valuable; and defined what worship is—loving God and neighbor with all our heart, mind, soul and strength. The daily devotionals focus further on the motivation and content of acceptable worship. This Bible study helps us to see God as of supreme worth, and what the experience of being a true worshiper is like.

Discuss

If you had a fire in your house, what three things would you pick up as you ran out of the building? What makes them so valuable to you?

> The aim of this discussion is to introduce the group to the question of what we value, and love. No wrong answers—just get them talking.

Jared said on the DVD: *"We worship what we most value."* Psalm 16 gives us a window into the heart and mind of David as he thinks and sings about his love for God and devotion to him. It will help us see what true worship looks like for a follower of Christ.

 READ PSALM 16

> ¹ *Preserve me, O God, for in you I take refuge.*
> ² *I say to the* Lord, *"You are my Lord;*
>   *I have no good apart from you."*

1. **What do verses 1-2 show us about David's relationship with God? What delights and excites him about the** Lord**?**

   - It is a personal relationship. God is not just God, but *his* God (v 2).
   - It involves prayer. *"I say to the* Lord*..."*
   - He takes enormous delight in God, but in a way that is exclusive—God is not just one great thing above many, but one great thing above all others. You might remind members of the *shema*, the Old Testament confession of faith quoted in the main session's DVD: *"The Lord your God is one..."*

2. **"I have no good thing apart from you" (v 2). What does this phrase tell us about how David sees his life and the world around him?**

- He knows that he has nothing good apart from God. God is the source of all good things—whether we acknowledge it or not.
- He knows that the alternatives are hopeless (v 4)—even though they might seem attractive or dramatic.
- He recognizes that everything that is good comes from God—love, beauty, gifts, life, pleasure and wealth. He is therefore thankful to God for those things.

How will this perspective help us when we are tempted to envy what the world has and enjoys?

David perceives that those who worship other things will only experience more and more troubles. People often worship things other than God because they think these will deliver happiness, satisfaction, salvation and other benefits. They may do, initially. David sees, however, that these things will not last... The devil's promises turn out to be seductive lies.

3. **List the blessings that God pours out on him in v 5-11. How does this help us see how valuable our relationship with God is?**

- v 5 *"Portion"*: He nourishes and feeds him. God gives each of us the spiritual food of Jesus Christ for our forgiveness—the "breaking of bread" service (the Lord's Supper, or Holy Communion) is a powerful picture of this. He also gives us the "daily bread" of his love, instruction and strength by the Holy Spirit.
- v 5-6, 11 *A home / a land*: He has inherited a place to live securely in. Believers are blessed with the knowledge that we are part of the kingdom of God—an international "nation" that is greater than any nationality we may have as citizens of a country. Our primary identity as believers is now as inheritors of the kingdom of God with Christ.
- v 7 *Teaching and wise advice*: We all need instruction and help to know how to live. In relationship with the Lord, we receive instruction from the God who made us and knows us, and who truly understands the way the world is. We receive this instruction primarily directly from the Bible, but also through the wise counsel of his people and from the inner witness of the Holy Spirit in our lives.
- v 8 *Confidence and security*: Because he knows God is always with him, he experiences an incredible sense of security. He is convinced of the sovereignty of God, and therefore can trust the Lord even when things are

difficult and hard. We can know this sense of confidence in our forgiveness in Christ, and in God's providential care for us.

- *v 11 Friendship and joy:* God is present with him and gives him joy and delight. We can *enjoy* not just the fact of our relationship with God, but also the daily experience of it. And even when God seems far away because of our circumstances or other factors, we can be confident that in eternity, we will enjoy the full measure of what we only glimpse in part now.

4. How does the love of God toward David stir his affections (v 3, 9, 11)?

Interestingly, David's experience of God's love causes him to delight in God's people—*"the saints in the land."* When we value God rightly, we find ourselves seeking out and being moved by the presence of his people, who also value him rightly. Bring out the sense of gladness, joy, confidence, happiness and delight that David experiences (v 9). To know and worship God as David does is not solemn or dutiful, but full of joy.

Additional question: If we are not experiencing a faith like this, is there something wrong with us?

It is important to air this issue and talk it through. Some people will be able to say a resounding "amen" to this psalm and identify with many or all of its experiences. But others may feel that what it describes is worlds away from them.

- *It could be because they are not a genuine believer.* Find out what they are trusting in for their forgiveness and acceptance with God.
- *It could be that they are a backslidden or disobedient disciple.* Being disobedient to Christ robs us of our joy in him (see Psalm 51:12).
- *It could be that they lack assurance and teaching about their acceptance with Christ,* perhaps because they are ensnared in a legalistic form of Christianity. Encourage them to enjoy what is rightfully theirs in the Lord.
- *It may be a temperamental or personality thing.* God has made us different. Some of us experience greater heights and depths of emotion; others of us are more even or more downbeat in general. Encourage individual members to make allowances for this in themselves and in each other.

Note that churches also have a "temperament" or general culture of how they express their emotional response. *What is the culture at our church?*

5. **Verse 10 is quoted in the New Testament as being a prophetic reference to the resurrection of Christ (see Acts 2:25-28; 13:35). How does knowing the meaning of this verse give us greater appreciation of the surpassing value of God?**

We have the witness of the apostles and the Scriptures to the resurrection. David trusted God's promise to raise him beyond death; but he was also prophetically looking forward to the One whose resurrection from death is the way that we can know for sure that we too will live beyond death. (You could read Romans 6 v 3-5.) The value of what God has given us in Christ will never be more apparent than on the day of our death—and the day after!

6. **Like us, David lives in a culture that worships other gods. What does he understand about these alternative objects of worship (v 4)?**

He knows that these things must be "run after" and strived for, whereas the real God does not require us to pursue him; he is ready to love and bless us. David also perceives that those who worship other things will only experience more and more troubles—that what "another god" promises, it will not deliver.

How would the truths elsewhere in the psalm help David to avoid worshiping idols instead of the one true God?

David's God gives him so much more, both in the present and the future, than any other object of worship. David does not simply resolve not to worship idols (v 4b); he recounts the glory and worthiness of the LORD. As he compares what he has found in the LORD with what "another god" offers, there is no competition! We all worship something, and the way to ensure we are worshiping God is not only to seek to avoid idols, but to remember and rejoice in all that our relationship with God brings us.

Apply

FOR YOURSELF: Which part of this description of David's spiritual life seems furthest away from your own experience? Reflect on why this might be, and how you could grow in true worship with your heart, mind, soul and strength.

Discuss how to follow up on your thoughts from question 4.

FOR YOUR CHURCH: How can you encourage genuine heartfelt worship in your own church? What would that look like in your conversations, singing and how you spend your time together?

Handle this discussion carefully as a leader. Churches have a culture or temperament—what might generally be felt to be appropriate ways of expressing our devotion to Christ when we are together. For some churches this might mean ecstatic, enthusiastic singing and worship (which some will find intimidating and "over the top"). For others it will be a more dignified, serious atmosphere (which some will find passionless!). When invited to critique your church culture, members will inevitably think about how they relate to this from their own particular God-given temperament—"It's not lively enough for me" or "It's too noisy and emotional for me."

The key to using this question well is to encourage your group to think about how they can encourage genuine worship of the Lord in the gathered congregation, *whatever it is like*—to be a participant in worship, rather than a critical "consumer" of church. That will mean simple things like singing enthusiastically, making eye contact with others as appropriate, and encouraging each other to remember the blessings that God has given us in our conversations. It will mean delighting in the other members of the church, loving and appreciating them in practical ways.

Pray

FOR YOUR GROUP: Pray that you would encourage and teach each other to remember the goodness of God. Pray that you would be devoted to the Lord and supportive of each other. Give thanks for the aspects of God's blessing to you that you have particularly appreciated as you have studied this psalm.

FOR YOUR CHURCH: As your church embarks on this series examining what true worship means, pray that you would grow together in appreciating the all-surpassing value of the Lord, and that you would have a growing desire to worship him, please him and honor him.

FURTHER READING

If we have a desire to worship God aright, we must remember how great he is.
John Calvin

Resolution One: I will live for God.
Resolution Two: If no one else does, I still will.
Jonathan Edwards

Are you gripped by the mercy of God? If not, you will never worship him. An understanding of God's mercy to us is the fuel that energizes and empowers our worship in all parts of life.
Vaughan Roberts

Books

- *True Worship (Vaughan Roberts)*
- *Counterfeit Gods (Tim Keller)*
- *Knowing God (J.I. Packer)*
- *The Air I Breathe (Louie Giglio)*
- *Romans 8 – 16 For You, chapters 7 – 12 (Tim Keller)*
- *The Expulsive Power of a New Affection (Thomas Chalmers)*

Online

- *God Invites us to Enjoy Him (C.S. Lewis)*
  gospelshapedchurch.org/resources111
- *The Grand Demythologizer: The Gospel and Idolatry (Tim Keller, video)*
  gospelshapedchurch.org/resources112

LEADER'S REFLECTIONS

SESSION 2:

THE FOUNDATION OF
WORSHIP

WE HAVE SEEN THAT EVERYONE IS A WORSHIPER; AND
THAT SINCE OUR CREATOR IS MORE VALUABLE THAN
ANYTHING IN HIS CREATION, WE ARE TO WORSHIP HIM
ALONE. NOW WE CONSIDER THE FOUNDATION OF OUR
WORSHIP: WHAT INSPIRES IT AND DIRECTS IT? WHAT IS IT
THAT TRANSFORMS MERE ACTIVITY INTO WORSHIPING GOD?

TALK OUTLINE

2.1 ● What is the gospel? How important is it to our everyday life as Christians?

● **THE GOSPEL IS THE MOST IMPORTANT THING** *1 Corinthians 15:1-4*
  - The gospel is what distinguishes Christianity. Other religions teach things to do; Christianity teaches that these things are already done.
  - Only Christianity teaches that we're unable to obey commands in a way that merits salvation; we cannot earn forgiveness.
  - The gospel is the good news that God saves sinners by his grace given in the completed work of Jesus. This should be "of first importance" in our churches.

● **THE GOSPEL IS NEWS, NOT ADVICE**
  - The gospel is news, not instructions: the gospel is the news that Christ died, was buried and was raised (1 Corinthians 15:3-4).
  - Romans 11:6: The gospel "stops" when we start trying to do things to merit salvation.

● **THE GOSPEL DOES WHAT INSTRUCTIONS CANNOT** *Romans 1:16*
  - The gospel is news, but it's not just data: it is a power in and of itself.
  - True change comes from believing the gospel, not by receiving more instructions. It's by hearing, receiving, standing in and growing by the gospel that we're able to worship God, instead of ourselves.

2.2 ● **JESUS AND HIS GOSPEL SHOULD BE THE CENTRAL THEME OF OUR WORSHIP**

Every church should be a gospel-shaped church. Everything should be done as worship of Jesus, from counting tithes to children's ministry.

● **THE CENTER OF WORSHIPFUL MISSION IS THE GOSPEL**

Gospel-shaped evangelism is one way in which we worship. It's impossible to do this without words, because the gospel is news.

You can download a full transcript of these talks at
WWW.GOSPELSHAPEDCHURCH.ORG/WORSHIP/TALKS

THE FOUNDATION OF WORSHIP

● *Ask the group members to turn to Session 2 on page 33 of the Handbook.*

Discuss

What is the gospel message? How would you sum it up in your own words?

In this session we will be looking at why the gospel is the foundation of worship, so it's important that the group members are all clear as to what we mean by "gospel." The gospel message is the good news of Jesus Christ. Specifically, it is the good news that God's promised, all-powerful King, the man Jesus, died for our sins to reconcile us to God, and was raised to life on the third day. We use the word "gospel" as shorthand for this, but it is important to make sure that people understand what it is. We often assume that people mean the good news as just summarized when they are thinking something different.

NOTE: People are sometimes confused about the difference between the gospel message (the good news of Jesus) and the four Gospels—Matthew, Mark, Luke and John. These four historical accounts tell us about the life, death and resurrection of Jesus. They are known as Gospels because they are historical accounts of the life, death and resurrection of Jesus Christ, but the gospel message comes from the whole Bible, not just these four books.

How important is the gospel in the life of a Christian? In what ways?

It's likely the group will say the gospel is very important in the life of a Christian! But tease out *why* they think that. Some may say the gospel is vital because it's the way in which they have a right relationship with God. Others may focus on the need to be regularly sharing the gospel with others. And some may think that the gospel was vital in order for them to become a Christian, but no longer plays a large part in their day-to-day life. Don't spend too long discussing these ideas—just listen to what people say—as we will be considering this in more detail later on.

▶ **WATCH DVD 2.1** (9 min 51 sec) **OR DELIVER TALK 2.1** (see page 52)

* *Encourage the group to make notes as they watch the DVD or listen to the talk. There is space for notes on page 35 of the Handbook.*

Discuss

 1 CORINTHIANS 15:1-4

> ¹ *Now I would remind you, brothers, of the gospel I preached to you, which you received, in which you stand, ² and by which you are being saved, if you hold fast to the word I preached to you—unless you believed in vain.*
>
> ³ *For I delivered to you as of first importance what I also received: that Christ died for our sins in accordance with the Scriptures, ⁴ that he was buried, that he was raised on the third day in accordance with the Scriptures...*

What does Paul say is of "first importance"?

The message that Jesus died for sins, was buried and raised again—all of which had been written in the "Scriptures" (the Old Testament). This is the gospel message.

This session is called "The foundation of worship." What would Paul say that foundation is?

The gospel!

What phrase does Paul repeat, and what does it tell us about the Old Testament?

He twice says: "in accordance with the Scriptures."

Paul is saying that the Old Testament already promised and revealed what would happen to Jesus: that he would die; that his death would be "for our sins"; that he wouldn't stay dead but would be raised to life "on the third day." The whole Bible is about Jesus—Old Testament as well as New.

The word "gospel" comes from the Greek word *evangel*, which means "good news." The Christian message isn't a set of instructions—it's an announcement of news. What does Paul say that news is (see verses 3-4)?

- Jesus died for our sins.
- Jesus was buried.
- Jesus was raised to life on the third day.
- All of this was in accordance with what had been written in the Old Testament Scriptures.

The gospel is how I became a Christian.
The gospel is how I continue as a Christian.

Which of these statements do you agree with and why?

Both are true. The only way to *become* a Christian is through the death and resurrection of Jesus to reconcile us to God (ie: through the gospel).

But the only way to *continue* as a Christian is through trusting in Jesus to save us from our sins and enable us, through his Spirit, to follow him. The Bible talks about salvation in three different tenses. **Past:** "I was saved"—from the moment when I first trusted Christ, my sins were forgiven and I was sure of acceptance with God. **Present:** "I am being saved" (as in v 2) as I continue to trust the gospel (ie: "hold fast to the word") for forgiveness and salvation. **Future:** "I will be saved" from the wrath of God on the day of judgment. So I became a saved person by trusting the gospel, I continue to be a saved person by trusting the gospel, and one day I will enter God's kingdom as a saved person by trusting the gospel.

▶ **WATCH DVD 2.2** (3 min 12 sec) **OR LISTEN TO TALK 2.2** (see page 52)

✱ *Encourage the group to make notes as they watch the DVD or listen to the talk. There is space for notes on page 37 of the Handbook.*

Discuss

We easily drift into "law mode" (what we do) and away from "grace mode" (what Jesus has done). Can you think of ways in which that might happen in a Sunday service: a) in the songs you sing? b) in the sermon? c) in your conversations beforehand and afterwards?

a) If our songs are all or mainly focused on our own actions and responses and feelings, rather than having a balance of both praising God for who he is and what he has done, *and* giving opportunities to respond to his grace, then we are teaching ourselves and each other that our Christian lives are about what we do.

b) Over-emphasizing application in sermons and not showing how it flows from the gospel may leave people feeling they have been given a list of things to do, so that their conduct becomes motivated more by "I ought to…" or "I have to…" than "Because of the gospel, I want to / get to…".

c) Before and after a service, it's easy for conversations to focus on comparing our lives (*How's the family at the moment? What grades did the children achieve?*) or sorting out the practicalities of church life (*Can you join the hospitality team? When can you help with redecorating the church office? Have you increased your giving recently?*). We slip into these kinds of discussions more easily than we ask how the Lord has been working in our lives, what he has been teaching us through his word, etc.

Since the gospel is the foundation of worship, every aspect of church life should be motivated by the gospel. It should be our "reason for being."

Imagine that two people are working together to prepare the refreshments for after the morning service. As they brew the coffee and lay out the cups, one is worshiping and one is not. How is that possible?

This is a question about our motivation for serving. Both people are serving—but are they serving Christianly, ie: are they worshiping? The question to ask is: what is going on in a person's heart as they serve? Possible wrong reasons for serving may include:
- Serving Jesus to be "good enough" for him
- Serving Jesus to "earn" something from him

- Serving Jesus to "pay him back"
- Serving to impress others
- Serving in order to belong to the church family

Think about some of the ways in which you serve at church. What difference will it make in each case knowing that the gospel is your motivation for serving?

This is a great opportunity to apply the teaching from this session to each group member individually. Try to make sure that everyone gives at least one example of a way in which they serve at church—but don't expect them all to be able to answer the question for themselves, eg: if Tom isn't sure how the gospel can be his motivation for mowing the church lawn, the rest of the group can help him think this through.

Pray

 1 CORINTHIANS 15:1-2

[1] Now I would remind you, brothers, of the gospel I preached to you, which you received, in which you stand, [2] and by which you are being saved, if you hold fast to the word I preached to you—unless you believed in vain.

Read these two verses again. Use them as the basis for thanking God for all that the gospel has done and is doing in your life. Thank him, too, for those who first shared the gospel with you.

Think again about the ways in which you serve at church. Ask God to help you keep the gospel central in each one.

Pray for the church leadership, asking God to help them make godly decisions that will serve the gospel in your church family and within the local area.

DAILY BIBLE DEVOTIONALS

Remind group members about the daily devotionals they can do at home over the course of the next week. This week the devotionals take you through the whole redemptive story of the Bible, seeing how Old Testament history shows us our need for a Savior-King, and how God promises his people just that.

SERMONS

OPTION ONE: 1 CORINTHIANS 15:1-8

Jared focuses on part of this passage in his DVD presentation, and you could expand upon it in a longer sermon.

OPTION TWO: TITUS 3:3-8

This is the passage the Bible study is based on (see next page), which could also be expanded upon in a sermon.

OPTION THREE: MARK 1:14-15

This passage is not mentioned in this material, but is a concise summary of the gospel message from the lips of the Lord Jesus. In his life, death and resurrection:

- God's Old Testament promises are fulfilled.
- God's kingdom comes, is seen, and is opened to sinners.
- we are commanded and invited to repent (accept Jesus as our King) and believe in the gospel (turn to Jesus as our Savior).

If one of your Sunday sermons is to be based on the theme of this session, church members will find a page to write notes on the sermon on page 51 of their Handbooks.

BIBLE STUDY

AIM: The main teaching session this week looked at how the message of God's grace toward us in Christ is the foundation of true worship. The daily readings give a mini overview of how God's plan for salvation unfolds throughout the Bible. This Bible study reinforces the key message of the gospel, so that your group can be clear about the fundamentals.

NOTE: Long-standing believers may feel that the content of this Bible study is a little basic for them, but we have included it here so that there is complete clarity on what the gospel is. Our constant pressure is to see the Christian life as beginning by grace in our conversion, but then continuing by law in our ongoing walk with Christ. Only by constantly returning to the good news can we maintain healthy Christian lives. If you are using this study one on one with a church member as suggested on page 27, make sure the meeting is relaxed and encouraging. For further help with one-on-one Bible study, take a look at *One to One* by David Helm.

Discuss

Have you ever had a hard choice to make where you made a list of pros and cons? What was the choice, and what decision did you reach?

> Alternatively, you could do this as an exercise. Depending on your group, compile a list of pros and cons of one of the following propositions:
> - Buying a DeLorean sports car as your next vehicle
> - Going on holiday to Afghanistan
> - Investing all your money in one of two companies—one that makes smart phones; another that makes video-cassette tapes

Paul's brief letter to his friend Titus was written to help him face the pressures of false teaching and unruly members in his congregation. Again and again throughout the letter, Paul tells Titus to teach, and trust, the gospel of Jesus.

READ TITUS 3:3-8

> *⁴ But when the goodness and loving kindness of God our Savior appeared,*
> *⁵ he saved us...*

1. What uncomfortable truths about ourselves do we see in verse 3? Who is to blame?

We were:
- *Foolish:* In the Bible a fool is someone who acts as though there is no God eg: Psalm 14 v 1.
- *Disobedient*: Whether or not we acknowledged God, we did not obey him.

Because our relationship with God was in a mess, our relationships with each other were, too. We lived *"in malice and envy, hated by others and hating one another."*

It is our fault and choice, but it quickly becomes an inescapable enslavement. Our rejection of God affected our thinking (we were "led astray") and we could not sort it out—we were trapped by our sinful habits.

Do you recognize this picture in other people? What about in yourself?

Paul's language can feel overly strong, compared to the "nice" people we see and know who may not be believers, and perhaps to our own personal history. It is not that we are as bad as we can be, but that our passions are ruled by self-interest, rather than genuine love of others and the Lord. Malice is wishing bad things on other people. Envy is wishing good things did not happen to other people, but to us instead. Note:
- This is a good opportunity for people to "own" their own sinfulness with some honesty.
- We do not want to caricature everyone who is not a believer as "nasty," but our own experience suggests that this is not far beneath the surface in all of us.
- Make sure the group does not spend a long time pointing the finger at those outside, but rather uses most of the time to reflect on their own sinfulness.

2. What did the appearing of Jesus—his birth, life and death—both show and achieve (v 4-5)? Why is this such a surprise?

- He came to save us from the way of life described in v 3.
- He came to show us who the one true God is.
- His coming shows that God is good, loving and kind—the very things we are not (v 3).
- He came to rescue horrible, trapped, foolish, disobedient people—*us!*

3. If God were to make a list of pros and cons about whether he should save us, what would it look like? Why does he save us?

- A mass of things on the "con" side of the list
- Nothing on the "pro" side of the list at all that relates to us
- The only things on the pro side of the list would be the attributes of God mentioned here: he is good, loving, kind and merciful.
- The motivation for salvation comes entirely from God.
- God did not think we were, on balance, OK; or that we had potential. He knew we were the people of verse 3—and he had mercy on us because he loves us.

4. What incredible blessings does he pour out on us in Christ (v 5-7)? Discuss what each thing that God gives us actually means.

As you find the answers, take time to unpack what they mean:
- *Washing of regeneration (v 5):* He cleanses us from the stain of sin, and makes us alive again.
- *Renewal (v 5):* We are made new people (see 2 Corinthians 5:17).
- *The Spirit is poured out on us (v 5-6):* Christ himself comes to live within us in the person of his Holy Spirit; not just in small measure—notice "pour" and "richly." When God gives, he gives lavishly and without holding back.
- *Justified by his grace (v 7):* Justification is a legal term—we are made right with God; declared "not guilty" of the sins for which we are responsible. But we are not acquitted through lack of evidence, mis-trial or on some technicality; we are justified by grace—the free gift of God.
- *Made heirs of eternal life (v 7):* We are given an inheritance of wealth which we will enjoy forever with Jesus in the new creation. The "hope" we have is not a tentative, conditional thing—*"I hope it doesn't rain tomorrow"*—but a certain thing based on the sure promise of God.

5. **What should our new status as cleansed, renewed, justified, Spirit-filled heirs of eternal life lead us to do (v 8)? What results from this?**

- Live a life of good works.
- This is productive for our lives as a whole.
- It is also "excellent"—we are living life as it is meant to be lived, rather than in the way described in v 3.

What is the order of events in this passage about someone becoming a Christian, and where do "good works" fit in? Why is it so important to get this right?

Make sure that people are clear about the order of events:
Not a series of good works leading to salvation...
But helpless enslavement from which we are saved by grace, leading to a life of growing good works.

Unless we have this crystal clear in our minds, we will not see that God's salvation is as great as it is, and we will overestimate our own goodness and ability to get right with God. There is nothing pleasing to God in our lives before we are saved. But God is pleased with us because of Christ once we are saved; and we are then able to please him in the way we live our lives (see for example Colossians 1:10). If we get this fundamental truth wrong, we will ultimately fail to live a gospel-shaped life or become a gospel-shaped church.

6. **From what we have seen in this passage, what would you say to someone who made the following statements:**

• **"I am trying my hardest to do good things so that God will accept me."**

- God does not accept us on the basis of our goodness—because we have nothing to offer him. He accepts us on the basis of his goodness. If we think our goodness can merit salvation, we are not converted and are still in our sins.
- Being a Christian is about being saved and changed by God. What results should be a life of good deeds.

- "I don't think I can be a Christian any more because I have messed up so badly."

  - Not true—a saved life is evidenced by growing holiness and good works, but we cannot lose our salvation through sin.
  - Continuing in sin—and not caring about it—can be a sign that a person is not truly converted. But there are many people with tender consciences who worry unnecessarily about this. The question for them is not: "Am I living a perfect life?" but: "Am I really trusting in Jesus' death to put me right with God?"

- "Now that I am saved, it doesn't really matter what I do and how I live. Forgiveness is already mine."

  - Not true—the Holy Spirit in us will start to change us so that we do care about sin, and we will want to start doing good and serving others. It does matter how we live, because it pleases God that we reflect his goodness, mercy and love to the world.

Apply

FOR YOURSELF: Where would you place yourself in this passage: have you experienced v 4-5? Are you struggling to live out v 8? Or are you still in v 3? How will you help yourself to move forward, wherever you are?

FOR YOUR CHURCH: Churches can get so familiar with the gospel message that we assume it is there behind everything, and we cease to articulate it explicitly at meetings and with one another. What are the dangers in this? How can each member contribute to insisting that the gospel remain central to church life and worship?

Pray

FOR YOURSELF: Pray that you would understand, believe, receive and rejoice in the blessing offered us by the grace of God. Pray that you would grow in works of service that are pleasing to God our Savior.

FOR YOUR CHURCH: Pray that the gospel blessings you have in Christ would be the theme of your conversations at church when next you meet together.

FURTHER READING

The gospel centers on Jesus. It is about a person, not a concept; it is about him, not us. The gospel is both a declaration of Jesus' perfect rule, and an invitation to come under that perfect rule, to make him our Lord.
Tim Keller

The basic operation principle of the gospel is ... one of unmerited acceptance: 'I am accepted by God through Christ; therefore, I obey.' To truly understand this ... at a life-altering level requires that the gospel be explored and 'looked into' at every opportunity and in regular, systematic ways.
J.D. Greear

Man's only righteousness is through the mercy of God in Christ, which being offered by the gospel is apprehended by faith.
John Calvin

Books

- *Christ-Centered Worship (Bryan Chappell)*
- *What is the Gospel? (Greg Gilbert)*
- *The Gospel (Ray Ortlund)*
- *Explicit Gospel (Matt Chandler)*
- *Honest Evangelism, chapter 5 (Rico Tice)*

Online

- *The Centrality of the Gospel (Tim Keller)*
  gospelshapedchurch.org/resources121
- *What is a Gospel-Centered, Missional Church, and Why Do We Need One?*
  gospelshapedchurch.org/resources122

LEADER'S REFLECTIONS

SESSION 3:

WORSHIP AND GOD'S WORD

WORSHIPING CHURCHES ARE BIBLE-TEACHING CHURCHES, BECAUSE THE BIBLE IS GOD'S WORD. BUT WHAT SHOULD A CHURCH BE DOING AS THE BIBLE IS TAUGHT? AND HOW DO WE CONNECT GOD'S WORD TO OUR WORSHIP? TO BE A TRULY BIBLE-TEACHING CHURCH, WE NEED TO BE A CHURCH THAT UNDERSTANDS WHAT HAPPENS AS GOD'S WORD IS TAUGHT AND HEARD AND LIVED OUT. THAT IS WHAT WE CONSIDER IN THIS SESSION.

# TALK OUTLINE

3.1 ● Imagine the main teaching at a church involves watching a Hollywood film, and then picking up on some themes or scenes, and linking them to some Bible verses. What is good about this approach? What is not good?

3.2 ● **THE GOSPEL IS A BIBLICAL MESSAGE** *1 Corinthians 15:3*
- The gospel is the foundation of our worship. It is **revealed** to us by the Holy Spirit-inspired word of God: the Bible.
- The Bible provides the **context** for the gospel; Christ died and was raised "in accordance with the Scriptures."
- We must handle the Bible respectfully and responsibly.

● **PREACHING IS A BIBLICAL CALL** *Romans 10:13-15*
- People must call on Christ to be saved; they must hear about him to call on him; so we must preach Christ in order for people to hear about him.
- The Bible commands the faithful preaching of God's word.

● **WORSHIP IS A BIBLICAL RESPONSE** *Nehemiah 8:9-12*
- Our calling "on the name of the Lord" is a response to the calling of the Lord upon us. The pattern of worship is "call and respond"; we don't summon God—he summons us to believe in, obey and follow him. *Explain how the format or liturgy of your church service reflects this dynamic.*
- We should respond to God's word with both conviction and celebration.

3.3 ● **CHRISTIANITY IS A BIBLICAL LIFE** *2 Timothy 3:16-17*
- Christians should go to God's word just as humans go to water, because: (1) All of life is worship; (2) The gospel is to be the central belief of our worship; (3) The gospel is a biblical message.
- To turn our whole lives over to the worship of God, we will need the resources God gives us in his word.

● **CONCLUSION:** The early church "devoted themselves to the apostles' teaching" (Acts 2:42). So should we.

 You can download a full transcript of these talks at
WWW.GOSPELSHAPEDCHURCH.ORG/WORSHIP/TALKS

WORSHIP AND GOD'S WORD

* Ask the group members to turn to Session 3 on page 53 of the Handbook.

▶ **WATCH DVD 3.1** (2 min 34 sec) **OR DELIVER TALK 3.1** (see page 70)

* Encourage the group to make notes as they watch the DVD or listen to the talk. There is space for notes on page 55 of the Handbook.

Discuss

Marty told Susan that he thought the teaching at the church they had visited was somehow "backwards." What might it look like to do it "forwards"?

You may find it helpful to read the full quote from the DVD.

On their next Sunday, Marty and Susan attended a fellowship in the middle of their annual summer series centered on "finding God in Hollywood." Each of the "sermons" in the series examined a recent popular movie and the preacher mined its story for nuggets of spiritual truth that may be relevant to the lives of the congregation.

Marty and Susan talked about the service afterwards. Marty ended by saying: "I mean, to show long clips from a movie and then break in every now and then and give us a short explanation with a Bible verse here and there... Don't you think that's, I don't know, somehow 'backwards'?"

Don't let this turn into a debate about the pros and cons of using video clips in a formal teaching session in church. It is about where the "weight" of authority lies.

If showing long clips from the movie, supported by little bits of Bible, is "backwards"; then doing it "forwards" would mean keeping the Bible central and using the movie to support it. This doesn't just apply to showing movie clips—any illustrations we give, or visual aids we use, need to bring the focus back to God's word and the things he is teaching us through it. Films, drama, visuals, illustrations, etc. can all be very effective in helping people to understand and relate to the main teaching. But if people leave the service only remembering those, then they have become distractions rather than aids.

▶ **WATCH DVD 3.2** (9 min 48 sec) **OR DELIVER TALK 3.2** (see page 70)

* *Encourage the group to make notes as they watch the DVD or listen to the talk. There is space for notes on page 55 of the Handbook.*

Discuss

 **LUKE 24:27**

> *And beginning with Moses and all the Prophets, he [Jesus] interpreted to them in all the Scriptures the things concerning himself.*

"The entire Bible helps us understand the gospel of Jesus Christ, because the entire Bible builds up to, declares, or flows from that gospel." How should this affect how we understand any and every Bible passage as we read the Bible ourselves or listen to it being taught?

If we understand that the whole Bible, Old Testament as well as New, points to the gospel, we will be looking for that as we read it or hear it taught. In particular, we will come to the Old Testament in the light of the life, death and resurrection of Jesus Christ. It is easy to do this with some Old Testament passages because they explicitly point to God's promise to send his chosen King, the Messiah. With others, the obvious meaning may be about God's character, or his purposes at the time—but we then see that these were fully revealed in the sending of his Son to rescue us.

PSALM 95:6-8

> ⁶ *Oh come, let us worship and bow down;*
>   *let us kneel before the LORD, our Maker!*
> ⁷ *For he is our God,*
>   *and we are the people of his pasture,*
>   *and the sheep of his hand.*

Today, if you hear his voice,
   ⁸ do not harden your hearts...

God speaks to us through his word, and calls us to respond to him. This pattern of "call and response" is seen throughout the Bible. Psalm 95 is one example of this.

When we "hear his voice," what must we be careful to do, and not to do?

- We must be careful to listen to him, remembering that he is our God, our Lord, our Maker.
- We must be careful not to "harden our hearts," ie: to refuse to listen, to ignore him and to believe lies about him instead.

"In worship we are responding to God's word." What are some of the wrong motives we might have for coming to church or as we listen to the Bible being preached?

- We may come to church to meet others, to enjoy the singing, to do a "job" (eg: only coming because we're on coffee duty), out of habit, or because we think God will be pleased with us for coming.
- We may have high or low expectations of the sermon based on who is speaking, rather than expecting God to be the one who speaks to us.

In Nehemiah 8 we saw that God's people first responded to his word being read and taught by mourning and weeping, and then with joy and feasting. As Jared says on the DVD: *"The response to the bad news was conviction; the response to the good news is celebration."*

Do you think every church meeting should have the same "feel" to it? Why/ why not?

There isn't one right answer here. If our worship is a response to God's word, then the "feel" of our worship service will be shaped by that. For example:
- If we are being taught from a Bible passage about our sin, and the way we have turned our backs on the Lord, both personally and as a nation, then mourning and confession will be the right response to that.
- If we are learning about the new creation and how we can be sure of eternal life because of Christ, then praise, thanksgiving and joy will be our response.

- And sometimes, as in the days of Nehemiah, the Bible teaching will lead us to respond in both ways.

The important thing isn't the exact mix of mourning/praise/weeping etc., but that these things are in response to God's living word.

What different kinds of response should we expect when the Bible is being read and taught?

There are many! They could include:
- Praise: God is great.
- Thanksgiving: God has given us all good things.
- Conviction of sin: we have turned away from God.
- Confession: asking forgiveness for our sins.
- Sorrow: seeing how our world ignores its Creator.
- Excitement: seeing how God's purposes are being worked out.

How does your church make space for these? Are any of them discouraged?

Discuss whether your worship services include a specific time to respond to the Bible teaching. How about at other times and places where the Bible is taught or read together (eg: small group, prayer meeting)?

Are some kinds of response discouraged? For example, what reaction would people get if they started weeping during the sermon?!

▶ **WATCH DVD 3.3** (3 min 3 sec) **OR DELIVER TALK 3.3** (see page 70)

✴ *Encourage the group to make notes as they watch the DVD or listen to the talk. There is space for notes on page 58 of the Handbook.*

Discuss

What opportunities for listening to God's word do you have during a typical week?

Think of as many as you can. This may include Sunday services, mid-week fellowship, homegroup, prayer meeting, prayer partnerships, personal devotionals, listening to podcasts of Bible passages or sermons…

How might you give yourself time and space to respond better to God's call in his word?

The answer to this may simply be to make a point of building in time. If we always expect God to be speaking to us through his word, then we will build in time to reflect on what he is saying and to respond to him. We need to remind ourselves that it is the work of the Holy Spirit in our lives that will enable us to both understand and respond.

Pray

2 TIMOTHY 3:16-17

16 All Scripture is breathed out by God and profitable for teaching, for reproof, for correction, and for training in righteousness, 17 that the man of God may be complete, equipped for every good work.

Spend some time thanking God for giving us his word.

Ask God to help you listen to his word, both as individuals and as the church family together, expecting him to call you to a response.

Ask him to help you respond gladly to all he calls you to believe and do.

DAILY BIBLE DEVOTIONALS

This week's daily Bible devotionals study six New Testament passages in which God calls us to respond to the gospel of Jesus Christ in different ways.

SERMONS

OPTION ONE: NEHEMIAH 8:1-12

This is one of the passages Jared looks at in his DVD presentation, which could be expanded upon in a sermon.

OPTION TWO: 2 TIMOTHY 3:14 – 4:8

This is the passage the Bible study is based on (see next page), which could also be expanded upon in a sermon.

OPTION THREE: PSALM 119:169-176

This passage is not mentioned in this material, but is a great way to focus on and enjoy the truths of God's word:
- What it is: God's statutes, commandments, precepts, law and rules.
- What it does: gives understanding, delivers us, teaches us, helps us and draws us back to God.
- How we respond to its call: praise God, sing of his word, choose to obey and delight in it.

If one of your Sunday sermons is to be based on the theme of this session, church members will find a page to write notes on the sermon on page 71 of their Handbooks.

BIBLE STUDY

AIM: In the main teaching session this week, we looked at how our worship of God is a response to his call to us in the message of the gospel through every page of the Bible. The daily readings looked at some of the different kinds of worshipful responses we are called to make by the message about Jesus Christ. In this Bible study, we focus on the centrality of the word of God to our lives as believers, and its central place in our gatherings.

This session will cover many things that evangelicals might consider "basic"—but it is wise never to presume that members of your Bible-study group share an understanding of the authority and centrality of Scripture. For those who may be shaky on the basics, spend your time working on them. If you have a group that is solid on foundations, spend more time digging into what our response should be, and how we can shape church life and our individual lives more helpfully around this principle.

Discuss

What is your earliest memory of hearing a Bible story? Who told it to you, and what did you think about it at the time?

Allow people the time to talk about what story sticks in their mind.
Any connection you can make between their belief in the story and the trustworthiness of the storyteller is a bonus!

Paul is writing to his young protégé Timothy, who was a church leader in Ephesus, encouraging him to keep going in the face of false teaching and persecution. As Paul finishes his letter, he underlines the central importance of the Bible.

 READ 2 TIMOTHY 3:14 – 4:8

[14] But as for you, continue in what you have learned and have firmly believed, knowing from whom you learned it [15] and how from childhood you have been acquainted with the sacred writings, which are able to make you wise for salvation through faith in Christ Jesus.

1. How did Timothy learn about the God he now serves in Ephesus?

From his family, who taught him from the Scriptures (Old Testament), and latterly from Paul.

How does knowing the people from whom he learned the gospel help him to trust it (cast your eyes over 3:1-13 for the context)?

- He knows the lives of those who taught him—he sees what believing God's word does to the character and priorities of those who believe it. Their godly lives show that God's word creates a harvest of righteousness.
- He sees that Paul has worked hard and selflessly for the gospel (v 10) and has suffered persecution (v 11). But he has also seen that false teachers teach others from false, selfish motives (v 1-9).

2. What benefits come out of reading and believing the Bible (v 15-17)?

- It can make us wise for salvation in Christ Jesus.
- It teaches us.
- It corrects and reproves us.
- It trains us in righteousness.
- It makes us "complete."
- It equips us for ministry and good living.

What difference is there between the benefits Paul lists in v 17? Why are they all important?

- The Bible gives us *wisdom*—the understanding and insight to discover and embrace our salvation. This is different from knowledge. "Knowledge is knowing that a tomato is a fruit: wisdom is knowing not to put it in a fruit salad." Similarly, knowledge is knowing that Jesus died for our sins: wisdom is putting our trust in that provision rather than in our own efforts.
- *Teaching* implies understanding things about God's character and purposes. But the Bible is not just a book of knowledge; it aims to change and shape us.
- *Reproof* is showing us how we are living and thinking wrongly.
- *Correcting* shows us how to live and think rightly.
- It does not just inform; it *trains* us practically to live for God—it gives us a specific skillset for godly living.
- All these things are vital, if we are to be equipped to worship God with our lives.

3. **How is the Bible able to do such remarkable things for and in us? How does the breathing image of v 16 help us to trust the Bible's authority?**

It contains the message about Jesus. It is all breathed out by God—it is organically derived from God himself. The word "breathed" alludes to the role of God's Spirit in the formation of the Scriptures. We often talk of the Bible as "inspired" but this verse tells us the opposite—it is not "inspired people" who wrote it, but rather, it is directly "expired" (breathed out) by God. As it is from God, it will display God's attributes of truthfulness, faithfulness and love.

4. **What will people in churches in every era always be tempted to do (see 4:3-4)? Given what Scripture is and does, why do you think this is?**

- We look for teachers that back up our own point of view.
- We have "itching ears"—we look for people who meet our perceived needs.
- We will always be tempted to gravitate toward teachers who agree with what we think, and who confirm our own wishes. We will be tempted to shape God in our own image, rather than be shaped by him.
- No one likes being reproved and corrected, and we have a natural, sinful dislike of authority over us. We will therefore always struggle to accept it.

What signs do you see of this today? When might you be tempted to do the same?

It's important that this question doesn't become an opportunity to criticize other people and churches without turning our attention to ourselves.

5. **How does Paul advise Timothy to work against this tendency (4:2)? Why is each part of his instructions important for his ministry to be effective?**

- *Preach the word:* People need to hear the message repeatedly.
- *In season and out:* Implying that Timothy needs to do it when it is easy and when it is hard.
- *Reprove:* He should continue to do the things in his preaching that the Bible itself does, ie: don't be tempted to strip out the hard bits.
- *Rebuke:* Preaching is not done in a relational vacuum—it involves relationships that challenge us personally. But rebukes must be seen to come from the word, not as personal judgments on our brothers or sisters.
- *Exhort:* The Bible is passionate in its appeal to us. So our preaching should be too.

- *With patience:* We do not "preach and run," but stick at it, praying that God will do his work through the word.
- *With teaching:* We are to give sound, rational reasons for what we are calling people to, and not just state commands and demand obedience. That we are teaching suggests that we are helping people to see and understand the whole counsel of God.

6. **What is our part in allowing God to do his work in us as we open up the Bible?**

- We need to put ourselves in a place where we will hear God's word preached by trusted teachers.
- We should recognize that we will be tempted to turn away from correction and seek alternatives.
- We should recognize that as the word of God shapes us, it will work toward making us complete. We should hunger for the maturity it will bring us, even though that may be painful to reach.
- We should hunger to be taught, so that we can understand and appreciate the gospel reasons why we should change and grow.
- We should depend upon the Holy Spirit's work in us for understanding God's word and having the power to change. Our hearing should be soaked in prayer.
- We should support those who teach well what God says to us, and who make us feel thrilled by the gospel and challenged about our response.

Apply

FOR YOURSELF: Review the times when you read or listen to Bible teaching each week. How do you give yourself a proper opportunity to respond to God's word, rather than just listening to it? What can you change that will help you grow in this?

It might be that you need to listen to more of the Bible, either through a daily devotional or quiet time, or through attending other Bible studies or church meetings where the Bible is preached. Or it might also mean listening to less of the Bible, but in a more purposeful way—focusing on applying God's word to our lives, rather than just listening to larger quantities of teaching.

FOR YOUR CHURCH: How can you positively affirm your leaders as they follow the pattern of ministry that Paul outlines for Timothy here? What things might help your church to be changed by God's word, rather than just being consumers of sermons?

Preachers will be affirmed if you tell them that you enjoy being taught from the Bible, that you have been challenged by their talk and are trying to work out how to respond, or that it has helped you with an issue you are struggling with.

Pray

FOR YOUR GROUP: Pray that God's word would have its effect on you, and that you would submit to its reproofs and correction, and pay attention to its teaching.

FOR YOUR CHURCH: Ask the Lord to help your church leaders be focused on preaching—and all that this involves—patiently, relationally, faithfully and fearlessly.

FURTHER READING

The most important thing a pastor does is stand in a pulpit every Sunday and say, 'Let us worship God.' If that ceases to be the primary thing I do in terms of my energy, my imagination, and the way I structure my life, then I no longer function as a pastor.
Eugene Peterson

The most valuable thing the psalms do for me is to express the same delight in God which made David dance.
C.S. Lewis

Worship is the believer's response of all that they are—mind, emotions, will, body— to what God is and says and does.
Warren Wiersbe

Books
- *Taking God at His Word* (Kevin Deyoung)
- *Can we Really Trust the Bible?* (Barry Cooper)
- *Expositional Preaching* (David Helm)
- *Creature of the Word* (Matt Chandler, Eric Geiger & Josh Patterson)

For Daily Devotional Bible Reading
- *For the Love of God* (Don Carson)
- *Explore: For your Daily Walk with God* (Various, search for "Explore Daily Devotional")

Online
- *Six Reasons Not to Abandon Expository Preaching* gospelshapedchurch.org/resources131
- *Is Preaching Still Relevant?* (video) gospelshapedchurch.org/resources132

LEADER'S REFLECTIONS

SESSION 4:

THE WORSHIP SERVICE

WORSHIP IS WHOLE-LIFE, JOYFUL OBEDIENCE TO AND
LOVE OF GOD, IN RESPONSE TO THE GOSPEL, WHICH WE
ARE TAUGHT THROUGHOUT HIS WORD. THEREFORE, OUR
WORSHIP IS MORE THAN OUR "WORSHIP SERVICES." BUT
EQUALLY, IT IS NOT LESS. THE BIBLE HAS MUCH TO SAY
ABOUT HOW WE WORSHIP WHEN WE GATHER AS CHURCH;
IN THIS SESSION, WE WILL SEE HOW OUR SERVICES
SHOULD BE SHAPED BY GOD'S WORD SO THAT THEY
BRING GLORY TO HIM AND BUILD UP HIS PEOPLE.

# TALK OUTLINE

4.1 ● Imagine a church that is formal and reverent but joyless. What would be good about such a church? What would be not so good?

4.2 ● **THE SERVICE IS FOR GATHERING THE CHURCH** *Acts 2:41-47*
   - The church gathering is primarily for **believers**. Non-Christians should be made welcome, but evangelism mainly takes place *outside* of the gathering.
   - The gathering is not a once-a-week pick-me-up. It's the natural culmination of day-by-day life spent together in community, as a body.
   - It is to feature teaching, prayer, breaking of bread, praise and giving.
   - 1 Corinthians 14:33: The worship service should have order.
   - Hebrews 10:24-25: The church should meet regularly.

4.3 ● **THE SERVICE IS FOR WORSHIPING THE LORD** *Psalm 96:7; 95:6*
   - The early church's "awe" and worship erupted from the gospel of grace.
   - The worship service exists to worship God! *Give examples of how aspects of your service put the focus on God, with reverence, sincerity and joy.*

● **THE SERVICE IS FOR REMEMBERING THE GOSPEL** *Acts 2:41-47*
   - In this passage, we see last week's "call and response" pattern. This grows into a beautiful church-building cycle: the gospel gathers people in by conversion; believers respond by devoting themselves to the teaching that won them to Christ; this devotion to the gospel draws more people in.
   - The gathering should re-center us on the gospel, primarily through the sermon, but also through participation in baptism and the Lord's supper.

● **THE SERVICE IS FOR SHAPING THE CHURCH** *Colossians 3:16*
   As we focus on celebrating God and his gospel, we will be spiritually transformed—individually, and as a community.

● **THE SERVICE IS FOR SENDING ON MISSION** *Acts 2:41-47*
   A gospel-formed community is a compelling witness, and our gathering equips us for when we "scatter" to share the good news with others.

 You can download a full transcript of these talks at
WWW.GOSPELSHAPEDCHURCH.ORG/WORSHIP/TALKS

THE WORSHIP SERVICE

* *Ask the group members to turn to Session 4 on page 73 of the Handbook.*

▶ **WATCH DVD 4.1** (4 min 9 sec) **OR DELIVER TALK 4.1** (see page 88)

* *Encourage the group to make notes as they watch the DVD or listen to the talk. There is space for notes on page 75 of the Handbook.*

Discuss

What was the best regular church service you have ever been to? What made it so memorable for you?

You can do this question before showing the video segment if that works better for you. The aim is to get people thinking about what they particularly appreciate about a church meeting.

NOTE: The three DVD segments are 17 minutes long in total, and there will be plenty of discussion in the rest of this session, so you may want to skip this first question entirely if time is tight.

What dilemma are Marty and Susan facing about their choice of church?

They recognize that they need "meat" (ie: good, solid Bible teaching), and a church culture that is firmly based on the Bible and serious about its calling and purpose. But they are also looking for a church that is stimulating and connected with the realities of everyday life, and that has a joyful expression of the good news they have embraced in the gospel.

Do you think their criticisms of the church they attended are fair or unfair? Why?

You may find that people are divided on this one. Some people temperamentally and culturally lean toward a sober and serious form of meeting/worship, and believe that this kind of cultural conservatism is more honoring to God. Others will assert that Marty and Susan have made a very fair criticism. Worship should be filled with joy and excitement at the goodness of God shown to us in the gospel.

▶ **WATCH DVD 4.2** (6 min 23 sec) **OR DELIVER TALK 4.2** (see page 88)

* *Encourage the group to make notes as they watch the DVD or listen to the talk. There is space for notes on page 76 of the Handbook.*

☛ **ACTS 2:42-47**

> *⁴² And they devoted themselves to the apostles' teaching and the fellowship, to the breaking of bread and the prayers. ⁴³ And awe came upon every soul, and many wonders and signs were being done through the apostles. ⁴⁴ And all who believed were together and had all things in common. ⁴⁵ And they were selling their possessions and belongings and distributing the proceeds to all, as any had need. ⁴⁶ And day by day, attending the temple together and breaking bread in their homes, they received their food with glad and generous hearts, ⁴⁷ praising God and having favor with all the people. And the Lord added to their number day by day those who were being saved.*

The Bible says a lot about the content, feel and focus that a church gathering should have, but very little about the place, style, duration, number of services and how much time each element should be given.

Think about one of your own typical church meetings. Which parts of it are essential? Which aspects are shaped by your own church's history and culture? Which parts are shaped by your local culture?

This conversation could go many places, eg: *Why do we sing so many songs that were written 150 years ago? Why do we sit in pews?* The essentials are shown in Acts 2:42-47. Apostolic teaching (ie: the Bible preached); lots of opportunity for fellowship, prayers and breaking of bread; praising; and displays of personal and practical generosity. But even these elements will be shaped to an extent by church or wider culture (eg: the length of a Bible-based sermon is not something mandated in Scripture!).

It is good to have elements that reflect your church history and local culture, so long as they are not an end in themselves. They are only of use if they serve the purpose that the church gathers together for. Otherwise they are deadwood that needs to be chopped off.

"For the early Christians, the weekly worship gathering was an extension of and a focus for the ongoing life of the Christian fellowship."

Why is it important for Christians to spend time with other believers during the week and not just during a weekend worship service?

- Being a Christian is an everyday thing. We need encouragement to live for Christ every day, so why keep it just to a Sunday?
- Christians are family. Loving families spend time together, and delight in doing things with each other.
- Our fellowship and love for one another is attractive to outsiders—it shows the gospel at work, reconciling believers to each other. Non-Christians should have the opportunity to see Christian fellowship in the normal course of life, not just in a "packaged" church meeting.
- Being a Christian is not easy, and we face temptations each day. Is spending a few hours once a week really sufficient for us to keep growing as faithful followers of Christ?

What do we miss out on if we are committed to attending the Sunday worship service, but not to anything else?

We miss out on daily encouragement; on opportunities to be a witness to others; on the stimulation of Christian discussion; and on opportunities to pray together.

Our meetings should be about the worship of God. How can we inadvertently make our meetings about something other than focusing on the Lord?

Even among evangelical churches, we easily become wedded to traditions or particular church models or programs, and lose sight of the purpose for our meetings. We can focus unhelpfully on:
- formal gathering at the expense of mutual encouragement.
- the personality and position of the preacher or pastor. He may be a "celebrity," but he is not Jesus.

- the quality/excitement of the music—whether that is modern with an electrifying band, or traditional with a choir and organ.
- "sound theology" and learning more intellectual truths about God, rather than encountering the living God together and worshiping him.
- running an "event" that is slick and professional, rather than gathering believers to celebrate God and the gospel, and to encourage each other.
- avoiding an error or unhelpful aspect of worship that we have seen in another church or tradition.

WATCH DVD 4.3 (8 min 45 sec) **OR DELIVER TALK 4.3** (see page 88)

- *Encourage the group to make notes as they watch the DVD or listen to the talk. There is space for notes on page 78 of the Handbook.*

Our gathered worship should reflect the gospel. What would an outsider learn about the nature and content of the gospel from the way in which our regular services happen?

- There should be joy, seriousness, thanksgiving, a loving family atmosphere and clear statements of the gospel facts, promises and commands.
- Invite people to think positively about how these different elements can be encouraged and grown if they are absent, rare, or not in balance.

What are some ways in which our worship service is or could be "outsider-friendly" without being too "outsider-focused"?

- Don't assume that people know what to do, eg: when to stand or sit, how to find the right page in a service book or look up Bible references.
- Give a clear and explicit welcome to everyone. Let them know what is coming up, assure them that they do not need to join in with anything they cannot do with integrity; and tell them roughly how long the meeting will be.
- Don't make assumptions about what people know. Explain the meaning of words and don't use Christian jargon without defining it.
- Explain clearly who should and should not take communion, and why.
- There should be a gracious, friendly atmosphere toward everyone.
- Sermons should not make caricatures of non-Christians, or make assumptions about their beliefs. When talking about "non-believers," assume that some of them are listening, and so speak respectfully.
- The only obstacle to joining in and belonging should be the gospel.

"We wake up each morning in 'law' mode." **How can the way we do church reinforce the view that Christianity is all about law and not grace—for both Christians and outsiders? What practical things can we do to prevent this?**

- Regularly remind the church family of the reasons why we do things.
- Always put love for God and love for one another together as an inseparable pair—the second flowing out of the first; the latter a natural expression of the former.
- Don't make people feel that they have done things "wrong" in the way that the meeting is conducted.
- Churches often struggle to find people willing to serve as volunteers in things like hospitality, youth ministry, etc. Appeals for help need to be couched in the right way so that people respond freely, not out of guilt.
- When we complain to each other, point each other to the gospel.

If you woke up next Sunday morning feeling like not going to church, what would you remind yourself about?

- "I need encouragement for today and for the rest of the week."
- "I need to encourage others—I am going as much for them as for myself."
- "I need to be nourished by the faithful preaching of the Word of God."
- "It is a gift and a privilege to be counted as one of the Lord's people."
- "Gathering together is an opportunity to worship God. He made such a sacrifice for me—here, I have an opportunity to sacrifice what I feel like doing, and in doing so to please him."

Pray

Pray for those who are responsible for planning and leading the worship services at your church. Ask God to give them wisdom in their planning.

Pray specifically for this week's worship service, including the preacher, service leader, the person doing the prayers, the Bible reading, the musicians, the people welcoming visitors as they arrive, and any others who you know will be directly involved.

Pray also for those serving behind the scenes by opening up the building, setting up beforehand, arranging refreshments, running the sound system, etc. Ask God to help them serve him gladly, in thankfulness for the gospel.

DAILY BIBLE DEVOTIONALS

Do encourage your group members at the end of the main teaching session to keep studying, or start to study, the daily devotionals. This week they take a more detailed look at the elements of the worship service mentioned in Acts 2:42-47: teaching, fellowship, breaking the bread, prayer, giving and praise.

SERMONS

OPTION ONE: ACTS 2:41-47

This is one of the passages Jared looks at in his DVD presentation, which could be expanded upon in a sermon.

OPTION TWO: HEBREWS 10:19-31

This is the passage the Bible study is based on (see next page), which could also be expanded upon in a sermon.

OPTION THREE: 1 CORINTHIANS 11:17-34

This passage is mentioned briefly in the devotionals, but nowhere else in the material, and is a helpful way to see the attitudes with which we are to come to our gatherings (and especially the Lord's supper):

- Unselfish toward our brothers and sisters (v 20-22, 33).
- Reverent focus on Christ (v 23-26) .
- Reflective honesty about ourselves (v 27-32).

If one of your Sunday sermons is to be based on the theme of this session, church members will find a page to write notes on the sermon on page 91 of their Handbooks.

BIBLE STUDY

AIM: In the main teaching session this week, we put the weekly gathering of the church under the microscope. We discovered that, while the Bible says a lot about the kinds of things we should do as we meet (teach, praise, pray, break bread, give), and the manner in which we do it (joyfully; in an orderly way; in a Christ-centered way; and intelligibly, in a way open to outsiders), it says very little about what form our meetings should take, the duration, etc. The daily readings encouraged individual reflection on each of these aspects of our meeting together. In this Bible study, we aim to reinforce how the gospel should be the heart and shape of our gathered worship, and to stimulate further discussion on the shape of our worship and our attitude toward it.

Discuss

What reasons do people have for going to church? Which are good and which are bad? Which of these is most compelling for you at the moment?

This is just a general opening question to get people thinking about motivation (what pushes people), and what draws them to a church. Some answers might include:

- To worship God
- To meet with other Christians
- To enjoy singing
- To take holy communion
- To listen to Bible teaching
- Because we always go
- To be with other people
- To meet my friends
- To escape from the pressures of life
- To have an experience of peace and beauty in a beautiful building
- Because I will feel guilty if I do not go
- Because my parents make me
- Because I am the pastor

Many of these reasons will be either good or bad depending on the attitude of the person who has them. Don't get into arguments about them; move swiftly on to the passage.

The letter to the Hebrews was written to a group of converts from Judaism who were experiencing persecution and had started to slip back into Jewish religious practices, rather than remaining distinctively Christian—some had even stopped gathering with other Christians. The author writes to remind them about the gospel—and how what they have in Jesus Christ is far superior to anything that the Jewish religion has to offer.

 READ HEBREWS 10:19-31

> *19 Therefore, brothers, since we have confidence to enter the holy places by the blood of Jesus, 20 by the new and living way that he opened for us through the curtain, that is, through his flesh...*

In the Old Testament, an elaborate system was set up to enable sinful people to get right with the holy God. The people could not approach God directly. They needed a priest to help them relate to God. The priest would make a sacrifice on behalf of people's sins and sprinkle the blood on the altar. The blood would turn away God's wrath against the sinner. Once a year on the Day of Atonement, after elaborate sacrifices, the high priest was allowed to go through the curtain in the temple to meet with God. For the thinking Israelite this raised problems. How could an animal atone for the sins of a human?

1. **Given this background, why are verses 19-22 so wonderfully exciting and reassuring?**

It might be useful to show a picture of how in the Jewish temple the "Holy Place" was separated from the rest of the building by a curtain. The writer is saying that Jesus has been a once-for-all sacrifice for us. His blood cleanses us so that we can approach the holy God. The writer is also saying that Jesus is the High Priest who makes the sacrifice of himself, goes through the curtain, and offers his own blood to turn away God's righteous anger against our sinfulness, so we can approach God with absolute confidence.

2. **How should Christians therefore approach God?**

- We can come to the holy God with full confidence that he will accept us by the death of Jesus.
- Make sure that the group understands what it means that God is holy— utterly pure and unapproachable by sinful men and women.
- We do not need a priest—Jesus is our High Priest.
- We come as forgiven sinners (v 22).
- We should remember that God is faithful (v 23).

3. **What does this suggest are wrong reasons for coming to church week by week?**

- Christians do not go to church so they can be forgiven. They are already forgiven.
- We do not need a priest/mediator other than Christ. The role of a pastor is different from the role of the priest.

So why do we come (see also v 24-25)?

- We gather with other Christians as forgiven children.
- To stir one another up to love and good works (v 24).
- To "[encourage] each other" (v 25)—specifically to keep going, and to remain faithful (v 23).
- The fact that "the Day [is] drawing near" (v 25) is greater encouragement for us to continue meeting in order to keep being faithful. "The Day" is the day of judgment, on which we will only be saved if we hold on to the gospel. Positively, it encourages us because the Day is drawing near—we do not have long to go. Negatively, our judgment will be all the greater if we let go of Christ.

4. **How do you see these aims for gathering as believers played out as you gather with other Christians week by week? How might these outcomes from our meetings be improved?**

- Praying, singing, responsive reading, and hearing the promises of God declared and explained in the preaching all encourage us to be faithful and keep going.

- "Stir[ring] up one another to love and good works" is perhaps less common in evangelical churches, maybe because we are afraid of appearing to promote a gospel of works, but love for neighbor is the necessary outworking of love for God.
- Our conversations can often be about the woes and difficulties we are facing. We should cultivate the habit of not just sympathizing, but connecting our conversations back to the gospel, and encouraging people to do good things, to keep trusting Christ, and not to slip back into old patterns of thinking and behavior.

Additional question: What questions can we ask each other in conversation, and what phrases can we use to encourage each other as this passage describes?

5. **Verses 26-31 give additional reasons for us to keep going as Christians. What aspects of God's character are we being reminded of here?**

- He is awesome and holy.
- He is a God of justice, and will punish sin.
- If we fail to persevere and be faithful, then we are in danger of falling into the hands of the living God—a dreadful thing (v 31)!

6. **As we gather to worship God together, how can we balance the truths of v 22 and v 31?**

- God is awesome and fearful, and the Judge of all mankind, and yet we are his forgiven, loved children.
- Somehow the character of our meetings must walk a line between awe and intimacy, between celebrating our forgiveness and the serious consideration of the weight of our sins.
- If the gospel is the foundation of our worship, we will not miss out the essential truths here—the holiness of God; the coming judgment, from which we need to be saved; and the glorious salvation that Christ has won for us.
- The gospel basis of our worship needs to be repeatedly articulated and made explicit.
- A careful balance of songs will bring across "both sides of the equation."
- No flippant talk about God and the gospel.
- But no grim joylessness either...

Apply

FOR YOURSELF: What one attitude will be different as you think about gathering with other believers as a result of this study? What one thing will you do differently at the next gathering of your church as a result?

FOR YOUR CHURCH: Do you think the character of your meetings leans too far one way to the exclusion of the other. ie: the awesomeness of God is emphasized, but the joyful intimacy of our standing in Christ is lacking—or *vice versa*?

Pray

FOR YOUR GROUP: Pray that you would continue to be faithful under fire, and that you would encourage each other not only to remain faithful, but to keep doing good to all people, especially the household of faith.

FOR YOUR CHURCH: Ask the Lord to help your church leaders be encouraging to the congregation as a whole, and that your meetings would reflect both the awesomeness of God, and the intimacy we enjoy with him through Christ.

FURTHER READING

Corporate worship is a regular gracious reminder that it's not about you. You've been born into a life that is a celebration of another.
Paul David Tripp

God is to be praised with the voice, and the heart should go therewith in holy exultation.
C.H. Spurgeon

Worship songs can't just be rooted in culture—they won't be deep enough. They have to be rooted in Scripture.
Matt Redman

Books

- *Rhythms of Grace (Mike Cosper)*
- *Worship by the Book (ed. Don Carson)*
- *Preaching the Cross (Together For The Gospel)*
- *Divine Commodity (Skye Jethani)*
- *Worship Matters (Bob Kauflin)*
- *Gravity and Gladness (DVD curriculum) (John Piper)*

Online

- *Better Church: The Why and How of Running Sunday Meetings*
  gospelshapedchurch.org/resources141
- *Gospel-Centered Congregational Worship: The Essentials (video)*
  gospelshapedchurch.org/resources142
- *Heart Issues for Worship Leaders (video)*
  gospelshapedchurch.org/resources143

LEADER'S REFLECTIONS

SESSION 5:

WHY AND HOW WE PRAY

CHRISTIAN PRAYER IS A GREAT PRIVILEGE, BUT IT IS NOT SOMETHING WE ALWAYS SEE THAT WAY. IN THIS SESSION, WE WILL THINK ABOUT PRAYER AS AN ACT OF WORSHIP. AS WE SEE HOW PRAYER IS DESCRIBED IN GOD'S WORD, WE'LL BECOME BOTH EXCITED ABOUT PRAYER, AND EQUIPPED TO PRAY WELL.

TALK OUTLINE

5.1 ● Do you find prayer a duty, a struggle or a joy? This session will teach us why and how we pray as Christians, both individually and together.

● **CHRISTIAN PRAYER IS RELATIONAL** *Matthew 6:9-13*
  - Jesus tells us to relate to God as our Father: he has adopted us as his children. We pray by the Spirit's power, through the Son's mediation, right to the Father's heart.
  - 1 Timothy 2:1-8: God loves it when we pray to him.

● **CHRISTIAN PRAYER IS RESPECTFUL** *Matthew 6:9*
  We can bring our real selves to God in prayer, but we must not come casually or flippantly. God is our Father, but he is still the perfectly holy Lord of all.

5.2 ● **CHRISTIAN PRAYER IS NEEDFUL** *Matthew 6:11*
  It is not wrong to pray for things that we want; but Jesus instructs us to pray also for the things we need. By praying, we acknowledge that we are desperate, dead and helpless without God.

● **CHRISTIAN PRAYER IS FAITHFUL** *Matthew 6:12-13*
  - Prayer is a spiritual barometer: if we are not praying much, we are not trusting God for much.
  - By praying for forgiveness and ongoing freedom from sin, we exercise the saving faith that justifies us, and we re-center our priorities on the gospel.
  - 1 Timothy 2:5-6: Paul declares the gospel in the middle of his instructions on prayer, because it is the gospel that allows and empowers prayer. We acknowledge this when we pray "in Jesus' name."

● **CHRISTIAN PRAYER IS MISSIONAL** *John 17:18-21; Matthew 6:10*
  - Jesus himself prayed that his Father would glorify himself in the saving of sinners through the work of his only Son.
  - The church's mission is to proclaim the gospel and demonstrate God's kingdom on earth; the church's prayer life should reflect these priorities.

You can download a full transcript of these talks at
WWW.GOSPELSHAPEDCHURCH.ORG/WORSHIP/TALKS

WHY AND HOW WE PRAY

* *Ask the group members to turn to Session 5 on page 93 of the Handbook.*

What are, or would be, the benefits of saying the Lord's Prayer together every week in a worship service?

- It's a prayer Jesus taught us and commanded us to use.
- It gives us a pattern for how we pray, so that we know we are praying about things the Bible gives priority to.
- In most western cultures, the Lord's Prayer is very familiar, so it would be easily recognized by many non-Christians visiting the church.
- The congregation already know the words, so they can be thinking about them as they join in (though see potential drawback below).

What are, or would be, the drawbacks?

- It can easily become something we say automatically by rote, rather than really thinking about what we're praying.
- Some of the phrases are complex and hard to understand if not explained.
- It can seem that by saying the Lord's Prayer we have done all the praying we need to (ie: we've "checked the box" by saying this particular prayer).
- It's not the only prayer we are given in the Bible.

▶ **WATCH DVD 5.1** (9 min 27 sec) **OR DELIVER TALK 5.1** (see page 106)

* *Encourage the group to make notes as they watch the DVD or listen to the talk. There is space for notes on page 95 of the Handbook.*

Discuss

 **MATTHEW 6:9-13**

> ⁹ Pray then like this:
>   *"Our Father in heaven,*
>   *hallowed be your name.*
> ¹⁰ *Your kingdom come,*
>   *your will be done,*
>   *on earth as it is in heaven.*
> ¹¹ *Give us this day our daily bread,*
> ¹² *and forgive us our debts,*
>   *as we also have forgiven our debtors.*
> ¹³ *And lead us not into temptation,*
>   *but deliver us from evil."*

"Our Father in heaven"

"When we speak to God we make him very happy. He loves it when we pray to him." (See 1 Timothy 2:3.) Does this statement surprise you? How does it affect our prayers if we believe this truth?

1 Timothy 2:3 says that when we pray: "it is pleasing in the sight of God our Savior." It is easy to see prayer as a "duty" or even as "work" that has to be done. But we will see it differently if we remember that God is delighted to hear us, and pleased when we pray to him. And what will particularly encourage us to pray is if we appreciate that God is our Father—he is all-powerful as he rules in heaven, but he delights to hear from his children. We don't pray to a distant King, but to a loving Father. Of course he loves it when we pray to him! And we can and should love it, too.

"Hallowed be your name"

"Hallowed" means "honored as holy." How can we come to God informally but not "casually"—being "real" with him but not irreverent?

There are a number of things that can affect the "feel" of our prayers, not just the words we use but also our tone of voice, our attitude and how we are standing/sitting. We need to be careful about these things so that we don't treat God irreverently. But neither should we let such reverence take us into a formalism that lacks a sense of familial love and closeness to God.

God is our Father, but his name must be hallowed. How can prayers in church express both of these aspects of our relationship with God?

When someone leads prayers in church, they are modeling the relationship Christians have with the Lord. Because of the gospel, we can know and approach God as our loving, heavenly Father. So we can come to him directly in prayer, knowing he is pleased to hear us and is interested in our lives—we can model this as we pray.

But our Father is also the sovereign Lord of all, the Creator and Sustainer of the universe. We will use language that reflects this as we pray.

▶ **WATCH DVD 5.2** (9 min 4 sec) **OR DELIVER TALK 5.2** (see page 106)

✦ *Encourage the group to make notes as they watch the DVD or listen to the talk. There is space for notes on page 97 of the Handbook.*

"Your kingdom come"

We are to pray for people to become Christians and for the gospel to grow. How can this be done sensitively in a meeting where non-believers are present?

One way would be to thank God for the gospel message, and for the joy and privilege we have in knowing him as our heavenly Father. We could then pray for any who don't yet know him in this way, or who aren't sure whether they do or not.

Avoid using words such as "pagan," "heathen" or "unbeliever," since most non-Christians would not think of themselves in this way, and feel insulted by it.

"Your will be done, on earth as it is in heaven"

God's perfect will is always what's best for individuals, families, the church, our nation and the world. How can we reflect that positively in how we pray?

Start by thanking God for knowing us so well and loving us so much, and for the fact that his will always is best. Thank him, too, that he is our powerful, sovereign Lord, which means he can ensure that his good purposes will come about. Ask him to help you obey his word, even when that's hard, and to trust in his goodness. When you pray for your nation or community, pray positively for them, asking God to help and guide them, rather than using prayer to bemoan the state of various ungodly aspects of society.

"Give us this day our daily bread"

"When we pray, we can bring our real selves to the real God to get real help for our real lives."

Our prayers can often be dominated by specific requests for things we want. How will understanding the difference between "wants" and "needs" help us to get a better balance in our prayers?

The things we ultimately need are all found in Christ. We need our sin to be forgiven; we need to be right with God; we need the Spirit to be working in our lives; we need the security of a certain future in the new creation.

Our daily needs may be things many of us don't often pray for because, if we are in the western world, we already have them—things like food to eat, somewhere safe to live, shelter at night… It's good to thank God for this generous provision, rather than taking it for granted.

It's not wrong to also ask God for specific things we want, but if that "want" is something we can't bear to be without, it has become an idol for us.

"Forgive us our debts, as we also have forgiven our debtors"

As well as confessing our sins together and thanking God for forgiveness, how can we encourage each other to be forgiving to those who sin against us?

In the Lord's Prayer, Jesus makes a clear link between the forgiveness we have been shown by God and the forgiveness we are to show to others. He makes this even clearer in the parable of the unforgiving servant (Matthew 18:21-35). We can encourage each other to be forgiving in the same way: by focusing on the enormous debt we owed to God, and that he himself paid by sending his Son to die for us—and then asking God to help us reflect his forgiveness in the way we forgive others.

Forgiveness is also "contagious." If we ourselves forgive those who sin against us, other Christians will see that and be encouraged to do the same.

Sometimes we need to encourage one another by directly challenging a fellow Christian to forgive someone else. We can easily excuse a lack of forgiveness without realizing it, but often it takes a brother or a sister to say: "Have you forgiven them? Why not? Remember the gospel and the forgiveness you have received," and to lead us to forgive people we struggle to love or who have wronged us in particularly painful ways. It is not easy to challenge each other to forgive—and it is risky to speak like this—but it is the loving thing to do.

"Lead us not into temptation, but deliver us from evil"

It's striking that, straight after asking for forgiveness, Jesus tells us to ask God to protect us from falling into further sin. How can we include this pattern in our prayers for one another, and for ourselves?

In 1 Corinthians 10:13, God promises to help us resist temptation: "*No temptation has overtaken you that is not common to man. God is faithful, and he will not let you be tempted beyond your ability, but with the temptation he will also provide the way of escape, that you may be able to endure it.*" This is a promise we can be sure God will be pleased to keep—so we can pray it for ourselves and others.

So we should not only name our sins in asking for forgiveness; we should name our temptations and struggles, and ask for protection when we face them. We should be proactive about our struggles (asking for help before they come), rather than only reacting to them (asking for forgiveness after we fail).

How do you think your church's prayer life matches up to the breadth and depth of the gospel-shaped prayer we have seen in this session?

Think about the varying places and ways in which the church family is at prayer, eg: in formal prayers during worship services, at prayer meetings, in small groups, in prayer partnerships, or when individuals are following a church prayer journal. Are there any areas of prayer that we've looked at in this session that are rarely included in any of these places or ways? Are there some areas of prayer that are always included—perhaps even too much?

What practical things can you do to ensure that each part of the structure given to us by Jesus is included?

Pray

The Lord's Prayer is often used as a "set prayer" (that we say together), but it is also a "structure prayer" (that shapes how we pray).

Use these different sections from the Lord's Prayer to pray for your neighborhood, your church, your group and yourselves.

DAILY BIBLE DEVOTIONALS

The daily devotionals this week work through Hannah's prayers of petition and praise in 1 Samuel 1. They show us that we can, and should, pray to our sovereign Lord about those things that are distressing us; that we can show our emotions to God without shame, but equally that we must approach him with respect as well as relationally, and with praise as well as petition.

SERMONS

OPTION ONE: MATTHEW 6:9-13

This is the main passage Jared explores in his DVD presentation, which could be expanded upon in a sermon.

OPTION TWO: COLOSSIANS 1:3-14

The Bible study is based on the second half of this passage (see next page), and it could be expanded upon in a sermon.

OPTION THREE: EPHESIANS 3:14-21

This passage is not mentioned in this material, but is another wonderful prayer of Paul's, which reminds us of:
- who we pray to: our Father, of whom every human family is a glimpse (v 14-15).
- what we pray: that his Spirit would enable us together to grasp more and more how his Son loves us, and how his Son dwells in us (v 16-19).
- why we pray: because we know our Father can and will do more than we even imagine (v 20-21).

If one of your Sunday sermons is to be based on the theme of this session, church members will find a page to write notes on the sermon on page 111 of their Handbooks.

AIM: The main session this week examined the subject of how our prayers should be shaped by the gospel, and the daily readings took a slow walk through the story of Hannah, gleaning lessons for our prayer life. In this Bible study, we'll see what gospel-shaped prayer looks like in practice.

Discuss

Prayer is a duty. Prayer is a joy. Prayer is hard work. Prayer is a mystery. Prayer is easy. Prayer is private. Prayer is to be shared.

Which of these statements do you agree or disagree with. Why?

> The aim here is to get people talking about their experience of prayer, and their general attitude toward it. You will get a variety of answers to this. Note what people say—especially those you think may be really struggling with their prayer life—and ask some "extending questions" to tease out what they mean by their answers. "Why do you think that?" "What do you mean by that?" "Has your view on that changed over time?"

The Bible is full of examples of people praying and their prayers. We're going to look into Paul's prayer life to see what we can discover about how to pray as a church family.

 READ COLOSSIANS 1:9-14

> *And so, from the day we heard, we have not ceased to pray for you, asking that you may be filled with the knowledge of his will in all spiritual wisdom and understanding.*

Paul heard about the faith of the believers in Colossae, who had responded to the message through Epaphras (v 7). He writes to them to encourage them in their faith, and starts by sharing what he is praying for them.

1. **What does Paul pray for the Christians in Colossae (v 9)? What do these phrases mean, do you think?**

   He prays:
   - that they would be "filled with the knowledge of his will"; that is, that they will understand the nature and character of God, and how and to what purpose he is at work in the world. This describes someone who has real understanding about God, the gospel and the whole message of the Bible from beginning to end.
   - that they would have "all spiritual wisdom and understanding." In other words, this is not just knowing and memorizing a series of facts; it is understanding how this impacts the way we think and live.

2. **What should this "knowledge" lead on to (v 10)? What do these phrases mean—give practical examples?**

   - "Walk[ing] in a manner worth of the Lord." "Worthy" means "worshipfully" —our lives are bearing witness to the value we place on God. So worthy, worshipful lives will be ones that are obedient to the Lord, and show his love and grace to others.
   - "Bearing fruit in every good work, fully pleasing to him." The knowledge of God leads on to practicing God's love, generosity and grace toward all people, especially the household of faith (see Galatians 6:10). Make the connection again between this and Jesus' greatest commandment: love God and love others. Both are intimately interconnected, and without the other each is empty (see Matthew 22:37-40; 1 John 4:20-21).
   - Encourage the group to get very practical about what this means. Personal holiness, yes; but also active involvement with both other Christians and other people.

3. **What else does he pray for them (v 11-12)? What do these phrases mean— give practical examples?**

   - He prays that they would be "strengthened with power ... for all endurance and patience." The power he asks for is to keep going—not necessarily for some mighty work or inner experience—but to keep at serving God, loving others and pleasing the Lord in the face of grinding opposition.
   - We see this in people who remain godly in the face of obstacles: the single parent who remains faithful despite managing a house, children and several

jobs; the couple struggling with young children and lack of sleep who keep working on their outreach and hospitality; those who care for an aged parent, and do not crumple or complain; the single person who does not give in to the pressure to date a non-Christian; the teenager who is laughed at for her faith at school, but keeps going; the student who refuses to join in with the debauched culture of their college. It can look a bit ordinary, and can feel like failure for those going through it, but it is the mighty power of God working in their lives.

- He prays for endurance "with joy"; not just enduring but with a deep-rooted delight in God, knowing that, even though life may be tough, we are truly blessed by God
- He prays "giving thanks." Gratitude is a mark of someone who is growing into maturity in Christ—we do not look at our problems, but thank God for his gifts in all things.

4. What effects of the gospel in their lives does Paul give thanks for in v 12-13?

The gospel has saved us from death to life; from darkness to light; from a hostile, doomed dominion to the kingdom of God's son; from slavery to freedom (redemption); from guilt and judgment to forgiveness; from poverty to a staggering inheritance. The essence of his prayer is that they would understand and enjoy what God has done for them in the gospel, and live accordingly.

Point out that when we say: "in Jesus' name" at the end of a prayer, what we are really saying is: *I can only ask this of you because of the gospel*, and also: *I can be confident that you will hear and answer because of the gospel.*

What can happen to our prayers if we forget the gospel truths of these verses?

- We can start to look on prayer as a means of manipulating God.
- Our prayers become selfish and focused on asking for worldly things.
- We will lack confidence to approach God with our requests.

5. What are some of the things he does not pray for in this passage?

There are a huge number of answers to this, but guide your group to notice that Paul lists nothing about their health, circumstances, or the individual problems they face. Tim Keller notes: "It is remarkable that in all of his writings, Paul's prayers for his friends contain no appeals for changes in their circumstances." (*Prayer: Experiencing Awe and Intimacy with God*, page 18).

The implication is that these things are far less important than the main things he does pray for: that they would know the will of the God who saved them; understand who they are in Christ; and walk in a way that is fruitful and pleasing to him.

What does this tell us about Paul's priorities for his friends?

- Their spiritual welfare and growth is far more important than, say, recovering from a cold.
- It is more important that they endure suffering faithfully than that they are freed from it.

6. **How does this compare with the kinds of things we tend to pray for in this Bible-study group, our church, and in our private prayer life?**

We often tend to focus on what we perceive as "problems" that we face—especially regarding health and our fears/worries about our children. And specifically, we ask God to change our circumstances or heal us. That may not be wrong, but the emphases in Paul's prayer are for something completely different.

In church we may pray for other churches, for persecuted Christians, for national leaders and for the work of the gospel in the church. Paul's gospel prayer priorities should inform how we pray about these things too.

7. **How is Paul's prayer a helpful model for the way we pray for one other?**

- We should focus on praying that other believers would grasp the gospel in a broader and deeper way.
- We should pray more that God would strengthen them through suffering rather than remove them from it.
- Paul tells the Colossians not only that he is praying for them, but what he is praying for them. This is a pattern we should follow.

NOTE: Since this study is intended to excite and encourage us to pray, there are no "apply" questions; instead, encourage your group to apply what they have seen in this passage by sharing an extended time of prayer.

Pray

Use Paul's words to pray for each other, and for the rest of your church. Ask God to help you grow and deepen in your faith, and give you the power to endure.

NOTE: This study may raise a number of questions that people have in struggling either with the point and purpose of prayer, or more practically with how to pray. You might follow up any issues that emerge with the suggestion that people form prayer partnerships to encourage and help each other to pray. For answers to specific difficulties, there are some excellent resources on prayer to point people to on page 120.

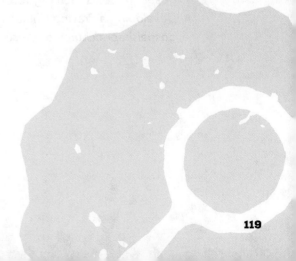

FURTHER READING

> *Prayer is that apparently useless activity, without which all activities are useless.*
> **Simon Barrington-Ward**

> *Human beings were put on the planet to depend upon their Creator.*
> **John Piper**

> *"Daddy." This is how Christians can approach the all-powerful Creator of the universe, who sustains every atom in existence moment by moment!*
> **Tim Keller**

Books

- *Valley of Vision: A Collection of Puritan Prayers and Devotions* (ed. Arthur Bennett)
- *Prayer: Experiencing Awe and Intimacy with God* (Tim Keller)
- *A Praying Life* (Paul Miller)
- *Bible Prayers for Worship* (Michael Perry)

Online

- *Public Prayer* (John Newton): gospelshapedchurch.org/resources151
- *On the Use and Importance of Corporate Prayer* (Mark Dever) gospelshapedchurch.org/resources152
- *Developing a Praying Church* (video) gospelshapedchurch.org/resources153

LEADER'S REFLECTIONS

SESSION 6:

DEVELOPING A CULTURE OF GRACE

CHURCH IS MUCH MORE THAN WHAT WE DO WHEN
WE GATHER ON SUNDAYS; AND GRACE IS ABOUT
MUCH MORE THAN WHAT WE HEAR IN SERMONS
ON SUNDAYS. ONE GREAT WAY TO THINK ABOUT A
GOSPEL-SHAPED CHURCH IS THAT IT HAS A "CULTURE
OF GRACE" -- THAT ITS RELATIONSHIPS WITHIN ITSELF
AND TOWARD THE WORLD ARE DIRECTED BY AND
CHARACTERIZED BY GRACE. HOW DO WE DEVELOP
THIS CULTURE WITHIN OUR OWN CHURCHES?

TALK OUTLINE

6.1 • Imagine trying to evaluate a church based only on its Sunday worship service. What would you miss?

6.2 • **THE MESSAGE OF GRACE DEVELOPS A CULTURE OF GRACE**
- A message of grace may attract people to our church, but it is a culture of grace that will keep them. Do we actually practice what we preach?
- Romans 15:1-7: A culture of grace starts with the gospel. *Give examples of what a culture of grace does and would look like in your church.*

• **SACRIFICIAL SERVICE DEVELOPS A CULTURE OF GRACE**
- Romans 15:1: Jesus set his glory aside to sacrificially save us; the church sets its own pleasure aside to sacrificially serve the lost and each other.
- John 13:35: Sacrificial service is a compelling witness to the truth.

• **ENDURANCE IN SUFFERING AND PERSECUTION DEVELOPS A CULTURE OF GRACE** *Romans 15:3-4*
- We must fix our eyes on Christ's willingness to accept pain and suffering.
- Suffering can cause bitterness; but endurance causes the church to flourish in spirit as it learns that God is good and trustworthy.

6.3 • **BIBLICAL AUTHORITY DEVELOPS A CULTURE OF GRACE**
- If we truly hold a high view of Scripture, we cannot and will not be legalists.
- Romans 15:4: If we submit to the Bible's authority we will: (1) proclaim the gospel; (2) hold to the hope of Christ's coming kingdom, and lose taste for the things of this world that make us self-centered and/or self-righteous.

• **MISSIONAL LOVE DEVELOPS A CULTURE OF GRACE** *Romans 15:2*
Churches tend to regard the world from the viewpoint of a consumer (using others to get what we want) or a combatant. But the church's posture must be one of missional love, seeking the welfare of our neighbors (Jeremiah 29).

• **CONCLUSION:** Where and how can our church develop a culture of grace?

You can download a full transcript of these talks at
WWW.GOSPELSHAPEDCHURCH.ORG/WORSHIP/TALKS

DEVELOPING A CULTURE OF GRACE

* *Ask the group members to turn to Session 6 on page 113 of the Handbook.*

▶ **WATCH DVD 6.1** (2 min 22 sec) **OR DELIVER TALK 6.1** (see page 126)

* *Encourage the group to make notes as they watch the DVD or listen to the talk. There is space for notes on page 115 of the Handbook.*

Discuss

Choose three words that you think describe the character of your church family. Would a visitor coming to a church small group or social event choose three different words, do you think?

> There are more questions than usual in this teaching session, and three DVD sections, so don't spend too long on this question. Tell your group to choose words that describe your church family, not the venue you meet in. Words might include: friendly, warm, serious, dedicated or fun. Visitors might say those things; but perhaps not! Notice the "visitor" in the question is seeing your church interact outside of a worship-service setting.

In this session we will be thinking about how our churches can and should model a "culture of grace"—reflecting God's undeserved love and kindness to each other and those around us.

▶ **WATCH DVD 6.2** (9 min 50 sec) **OR DELIVER TALK 6.2** (see page 126)

* *Encourage the group to make notes as they watch the DVD or listen to the talk. There is space for notes on page 115 of the Handbook.*

Discuss

"The message of grace creates a culture of grace." In what ways do you see this

happening in practice in your church? What might prevent this happening?

Remind the group that a "culture of grace" means "reflecting God's undeserved love and kindness to each other and those around us" (see page 115 of the Handbook). Ask if they can think of examples of that in your church. This may be at Sunday services, in midweek groups, or the way in which individual church members show love and kindness to others in the church or neighborhood.

God's love is undeserved—he loves the unlovable—so we need to be willing to do the same. Sometimes we don't reflect God's grace in our own relationships with others because:

- we are not willing to spend time with people we struggle to like, or we choose only to be with our own circle of friends.
- we may not be willing to forgive people who have hurt us.
- we are willing to serve and be loving, but only up to a point—or we subconsciously keep a score of whether we've been served as much as we have served others.
- we may want to keep a tight hold on our money, rather than share it with others (especially if we feel they don't "deserve" our help).

☞ ROMANS 15:1-3

¹ We who are strong have an obligation to bear with the failings of the weak, and not to please ourselves. ² Let each of us please his neighbor for his good, to build him up. ³ For Christ did not please himself, but as it is written, "The reproaches of those who reproached you fell on me."

Who are we to please and not to please, and why?

We are to please our neighbor—for his own good and in order to build him up.

We are not to please ourselves—because we have an "obligation" to those who are "weak." Also, we are to imitate the example of Jesus, who chose to suffer and die for us rather than to please himself.

"Just as Jesus set his glory aside to sacrificially save those weakened by sin, the church sets its own pleasure aside to sacrificially serve the lost and each other."

What "pleasures" might we need to put aside as church members in order to serve others? When do you find this hardest to do?

- We can be tempted to spend all our time with those we already know and like. We may need to be willing to spend less time on the pleasure of being with our friends so that we have time available for those who need our support.
- We may need to move to a new small group or divide an existing group (even if the group really enjoy being together) so as to make room for new people.
- We may need to accept styles of worship service or music that we don't particularly enjoy in order to give preference to those who have different likes and dislikes to our own. This means not just agreeing to such changes but deciding not to grumble about them!

In Romans, Paul tells us that "we know that for those who love God all things work together for good," so that we are "conformed to the image of his Son" (see Romans 8:28 and 29).

How can suffering make us more like Christ?

The Bible tells us that God uses suffering to shape us into the likeness of his Son (eg: James 1:2-4; 1 Peter 1:6-7). Suffering makes us aware of our weakness and the need to depend fully on God. We will need to trust in God's goodness and ask for his strength to cope. We will need to grow in our understanding of God's purposes, and ask him to strengthen our faith. Suffering also strips away things we may be tempted to put our hope in, so that we come to understand and appreciate how wonderful it is to be able to hope in God alone and look forward to eternity with him, just as Christ did (Romans 5:1-5; Hebrews 12:2).

How can we allow suffering to make us less like Christ?

We will allow suffering to make us less like Christ if:
- we become bitter about the things we are experiencing, or accuse God of treating us unfairly compared with others.
- we cut ourselves off from God (eg: by not reading the Bible or praying)—effectively "sulking" because we are experiencing suffering.
- we become proud of the way we are handling suffering, or think that God will love and/or bless us more because of our suffering.

How can we as a church both help each other to have, and hinder each other from having, a biblical view of suffering and persecution?

We have an automatic assumption that anything hard, difficult or painful must be wrong, and that therefore the right reaction is to do what is necessary to get rid of it or take the pain away.

Think about how we pray for someone who is suffering in some way. Do we only pray for the suffering to be taken away? If so, this can give the impression that suffering must only be a "bad" thing, to be avoided whenever possible, and that the best thing God can do is to take it away. But the Bible tells us that God uses suffering to shape us to become more like Christ. So we should be praying that the Lord will use it to work in our hearts to make us more and more like his Son.

This doesn't mean it's wrong to pray for relief from suffering or healing from illness. But we can do so in a way that recognizes that God uses suffering for his own good purposes, and that our need to know God better and grow more like Christ is more important than our desire to be well or to avoid hardship.

▶ **WATCH DVD 6.3** (7 min 35 sec) **OR DELIVER TALK 6.3** (see page 126)

* *Encourage the group to make notes as they watch the DVD or listen to the talk. There is space for notes on page 118 of the Handbook.*

Discuss

We may have a high view of Scripture, but how can we ensure as a church that we grow in grace as we hear and receive the word of God?

Having a high view of Scripture means much more than just believing the Bible is God's word, and making sure it is read and taught in church gatherings. To really have a high view of Scripture, we need to be eagerly asking God to change us by his word, and to be showing us how to live wholeheartedly for him. We will look forward to hearing the Bible taught, expect God to speak to us in our devotions, and want to tell others about the things he has been doing in our lives and church through his word.

In our relationships with the world, we can act as consumers or combatants.

- **A consumer is someone who doesn't really care about the people in the world, but "uses" them: to accumulate wealth, advance in their career, gain security and significance outside the gospel, etc.**
- **A combatant is someone who instinctively sees the world of non-Christians as an enemy to be fought and put down, rather than loved and blessed.**

How would your church find it easiest to act as consumers?

How your church could fall into this view of the world will depend very much on what your surrounding culture is like, and what other religious influences there are around you (eg: the "prosperity gospel"). Make sure that you discuss *your* church.

- Many people, including Christians, see the world outside the church as the place simply in which to accumulate and achieve. This can make us unhealthily separatist.
- As individuals, we can use the system to meet our own ends, and fail to see it in spiritual terms—as part of the blessing of God to us. Or in terms of our constructive participation in it, we can fail to see that it is a fallen system that we are called to be salt and light to.
- We can even be guilty of this in our evangelism. When we "just want to tell the message" to someone, and are not prepared to build a relationship of love that might be demanding of our time and resources, we are in danger of not fulfilling the law of Christ.

In what ways could your church fall into adopting a "combative" stance toward the world? What dangers are there in that?

- There are of course some things that it is right for us to protest about and take a stand on, but this is not an excuse for separating ourselves from the world and treating all non-Christians as "the enemy" to be avoided. This is another way in which we become unhealthily separatist.
- Is your church involved in prominent political and social campaigns over local and national issues? How much of your time and energies does this take up?

The prime danger is that we fail to have the time and space in which to love others and work for the blessing of the world if we are constantly fighting it.

The opposite of acting as consumers or combatants in how we treat the world is to love the world with the love that Christ first showed us. This is part of our true worship—because *"a gracious community makes Jesus look big."*

How might a "culture of grace" be encouraged to grow in your church? Be specific.

A "culture of grace" doesn't happen because church members decide to be "nice"—socially polite and kind, as opposed to truly loving and gracious in a Christian way. Such a culture only grows out of a deep appreciation of the grace that God has shown to us in Christ, and an understanding that his grace has worked in us to enable us, in turn, to show his grace toward others. This is why *"a gracious community makes Jesus look big"*—because it showcases his gracious kindness to its members, and to the world.

The starting point for any church that wants to grow a culture of grace is to be teaching the gospel faithfully and regularly, and applying it graciously and challengingly to people's lives together; and asking whether all of the church members have received God's work in their own lives (ie: they are Christians).

Additional question: Ask the group to name specific people in the church and neighborhood who need to experience gracious love in some way. If they can't think of examples, it will reveal the extent to which they are not involved in either church life or their community. What can they do to begin to reflect God's love and forgiveness to these people? If they can think of examples, are they proactively seeking to meet those needs? How?

Pray

Thank God for the grace he has shown you in Jesus. Be specific in your thanks.

Ask God to help you set aside your own pleasures to sacrificially serve others.

Confess to God the times when you have acted as consumers or combatants. Ask him to help you to replace these attitudes with love for the world, and especially for those in your neighborhood.

DAILY BIBLE DEVOTIONALS

This week's individual devotional studies take you to the first few chapters of the book of Revelation. They begin with the vision of the glorious, risen Jesus standing among his churches, or "lampstands"; take in the encouragements and warnings to his church, then and now, in chapters 2 – 3; and finish with the great vision in chapter 7 of the church in heaven, worshiping the Lamb, who died to bring them there.

SERMONS

OPTION ONE: ROMANS 15:1-7

This passage is the one Jared focuses on in the main session, which could be expanded upon in a sermon.

OPTION TWO: COLOSSIANS 3:5-14

This is the passage the Bible study is based on (see next page), which could also be expanded upon in a sermon.

OPTION THREE: 1 CORINTHIANS 12:12-31

This passage is not mentioned in this material, but provides us with a great picture of how we live as church. Each local church is a body:
- We are all different, and so we are all needed by the body (v 14-20).
- We all need all the other parts of our body (v 21-24a).
- We are placed in our church body by God, to identify with each part of it and use our gifts to serve all of it (v 24b-31).

If one of your Sunday sermons is to be based on the theme of this session, church members will find a page to write notes on the sermon on page 131 of their Handbooks.

BIBLE STUDY

AIM: In the main session we thought about how the gospel, rightly understood and applied, turns us into a community of grace toward each other and to all people. The daily readings thought about how that goes wrong in specific church situations. In this Bible study, we look at how gospel-shaped worship feeds into this culture of practical grace.

Discuss

What is the mood and feel you might get from a crowd at the following places?

- **A sporting event**
- **A classical music concert**
- **A New Year's Eve party**
- **A performance of Macbeth**
- **A state funeral**
- **Your regular church service**

Different gatherings are filled with different feelings: some somber, some joyous, some mixed. A classical music concert might be serious, but end in rapture as people applaud the performance. The idea is to get a sense of the range of feelings and emotions that occur as people gather together. Get the group to give one-word answers, or else this might take up the whole of your time!

READ COLOSSIANS 3:5-14

Put to death therefore what is earthly in you...

Paul has explained the good news of the gospel in the first half of his letter, and now goes on to draw out the implications of how we live together as followers of Christ.

1. **How did the Colossians once "walk" (v 5, 8)? What did they worship? (Hint: An idol is a false god we serve and worship.)**

- v 5: Sexual immorality, impurity, passion, evil desire and covetousness.
- v 8: Anger, wrath, malice, slander and obscene talk.
- They worshiped the things they desired (v 5: covetousness is idolatry)—this can be both possessions and people, as in the 10th commandment.

Paul uses the picture of putting off and putting on clothes to describe the change in us when we embrace the gospel (v 9-10).

2. Think about this illustration. How does what you wear reflect what you are?

- We can dress to reflect our mood or a special occasion.
- We dress to show the job we do (suit, uniform), or the character we have (casual, formal, etc.).

What are we to "put off," and why?

Talk briefly about the things that are no longer appropriate for a believer. Note that the "sins" listed are about our relationships with one another, and about our speech—the works of our old self, which is now gone. Those clothes no longer suit who we are in Christ.

What is exciting about what we are to "put on" (v 10, 12)?

We put on the clothes of Jesus' perfect character, because we are now being recreated in the image of God—we are becoming the people God designed and created us to be, made in his image (see Genesis 1:26-27).

3. How should they live now (v 11-14)? How is each of these qualities connected to the gospel?

- *No racism (v 11):* because Jesus is pleased to see people saved from every nation.
- *Compassionate hearts, kindness (v 12):* because God has been gracious and compassionate toward us.
- *Humility, meekness, and patience (v 13):* qualities that Jesus exemplified in his life.
- *Bearing with one another (v 13):* human beings just rub each other up the wrong way; we get irritated with each other, and divide. Remembering that our offence against God is so much greater, and yet that he continues to love us, can help us to be patient with others.

- *Forgiving each other (v 13):* "as the Lord has forgiven you."
- *Loving (v 14):* "which binds everything together in perfect harmony." We are told that God is love—it is the defining bond between God the Father, Son and Holy Spirit. To be loving is to reflect God's true nature.

In which of these do you think your congregation as a whole is doing well? Which need improvement?

4. What does it mean to "let the peace of Christ rule in your hearts"?

Note that here "your" is plural. When we act, speak and are motivated wrongly, it is because we have divided, selfish hearts (see James 4:1-2). The "peace" here is a solid understanding that we are now at peace with God—we are no longer his enemies but his friends, through the gospel. Paul says that we should allow the peace of the gospel to be the supreme thing in our mind and motivations (what is meant by "heart" here). It is not, in the first place, a feeling; but the fact of being at peace with God brings an experience of peace into our lives.

5. What does it mean to let the word of Christ dwell "richly" in us? How might it dwell "poorly"?

Again "you" is plural. It is not enough that we have a room full of people who know their Bibles thoroughly. We need to be sharing the good news of the gospel in all its fullness with one another.

To do this richly means that we do not reserve it just for the sermon. The gospel should be the theme of our conversations and interaction, and in the various kinds of singing we join in with. The word of Christ might dwell in us poorly if we confine gospel speaking to just the sermon, rather than making it the whole theme of what we do together. It will also dwell in us poorly if we do not allow it to affect our emotions and lifestyle.

The important thing here to note is the journey from the head to the heart. Knowing facts about God in my head alone will never produce the result of a changed and grateful life. "'Knowledge' puffs up, but love builds up," says Paul in 1 Corinthians 8:1. This is true not just for individuals, but for whole communities of people.

What will the peace and the word of Christ dwelling in us lead to (v 15, 16, 17)?

Thanksgiving: this is repeated three times to underline how very important it is. The overwhelming experience of gathering with other believers should be that we are enormously grateful together to God for the gospel.

6. What does it mean to "do everything in the name of the Lord Jesus" (v 17)?

Someone's name is their honor, their character and their person. The phrase means a number of things:

- To do everything because Jesus Christ has saved us.
- Name=authority. So there is a sense in which to do everything in the name of the Lord Jesus is to do it with his authority and power.
- To do everything in the manner in which Jesus would have done it.
- All the above mean that we will do everything to the glory of the Lord Jesus.

Apply

FOR YOURSELF: What do you struggle most to "put off" from your old life? How can we help each other with this?

What one thing could you do that would enable the word of Christ to dwell more richly in your meeting this coming Sunday? What about when you next meet up with some other Christians outside a formal church meeting?

FOR YOUR CHURCH: Often we will not need to be gentle, be kind, bear with one another or forgive one another—because our relationships are never deep enough to be in danger of needing those things. How will you become closer as a grateful and united group of believers?

Would an outside observer think that your church was marked by an outpouring of gratitude to God for his grace?

Pray

Pray that both you and your church would be excited to talk about the gospel and to live it out—in your church, family and work relationships. Pray that you would be grateful, gracious people.

FURTHER READING

> The highest form of worship is the worship of unselfish Christian service. The greatest form of praise is the sound of consecrated feet seeking out the lost and helpless.
> **Billy Graham**

> The church is Christ's answer to pride. Being part of a church encourages us, sometimes forces us, to not think about ourselves too much. It makes us think about others more. It provokes us to rely on Christ increasingly. It provides others to cut us down to size when we need it, and build us up when we need it.
> **John Hindley**

Books

- *Note to Self (Joe Thorn)*
- *Life Together (Dietrich Bonhoeffer*
- *Loving the Way Jesus Loves (Phil Ryken)*
- *Total Church (Steve Timmis & Tim Chester)*
- *Serving Without Sinking (John Hindley)*
- *Gospel Wakefulness (Jared Wilson)*

Online

- *Create a Contrast Culture in your Church gospelshapedchurch.org/resources161*
- *Brothers, Build a Gospel Culture: gospelshapedchurch.org/resources162*

LEADER'S REFLECTIONS

SESSION 7:

BEING
CHURCH

WE OFTEN TALK ABOUT "GOING TO CHURCH." WHAT
CHANGES IF WE START TO THINK ABOUT "BEING
CHURCH"? IN THIS LAST SESSION, AS WE CONSIDER WHAT
IT MEANS FOR US TO "BE CHURCH," WE WILL DRAW
TOGETHER ALL THAT WE HAVE BEEN HEARING FROM
GOD'S WORD ABOUT WHY AND HOW WE WORSHIP.

TALK OUTLINE

7.1 • Joining a church is a little like getting married: you never know someone deeply until you make that commitment! *Share an example of church family relationships overcoming sinful human nature and deepening over time.*

• **THE CHURCH MAKES A COMMITMENT TO LOVE** *Romans 12:9-21*
  • This is a picture of the gospel taking charge of church culture.
  • We should be so captivated by God's immeasurable love to us in the gospel that we make real, deep, lasting, loving commitments to each other.

• **THE CHURCH MAKES A COMMITMENT TO TRUTH** *Romans 12:9*
  • Christians live for the *church's* growth and reputation.
  • Holding to the truth means pursuing moral behavior *and* biblical doctrine. This is closely connected to pursuing genuine love.

7.2 • **THE CHURCH MAKES A COMMITMENT TO GATHER** *Romans 12:11-13*
  • This passage assumes we are frequently with one another! Church attendance on a Sunday is key but not the totality of Christian fellowship.
  • Refusing to embrace those whom Jesus has united to himself is selfish.
  • When we live with other believers in grace and love, we show how wonderful the gospel is.

• **THE CHURCH MAKES A COMMITMENT TO SERVE** *Romans 12:13-16*
  • We are to serve one another practically, emotionally and spiritually.
  • To do so, the gospel must humble us and the Spirit must empower us.

7.3 • **THE CHURCH MAKES A COMMITMENT TO BLESS THE WORLD**
  • v 17-21: The gospel overflows in outward acts of justice, mercy and blessing.
  • If we say we love God but do not love our brothers and the lost, we are liars.
  • Acts of blessing recollect God's grace to us and foreshadow God's perfect, eternal kingdom.

• **CONCLUSION:** We worship by committing to love one another and the world.

You can download a full transcript of these talks at
WWW.GOSPELSHAPEDCHURCH.ORG/WORSHIP/TALKS

BEING CHURCH

* *Ask the group members to turn to Session 7 on page 133 of the Handbook.*

Discuss

What can prevent people from being committed to a local church fellowship?

There are two levels to this question.

- First, what things can prevent someone from making an initial commitment to becoming part of a church fellowship? On one hand, it may be some of the things Marty and Susan have been discussing after their church visits: the preaching, music, welcome or small groups. On the other hand, it may be a lack of willingness to make a real commitment; eg: a consumer mentality, or searching for the "perfect" church.
- Second, what kinds of things may prevent someone from staying committed and cause them to become less involved over time? For example, difficult relationships with other church members, not getting involved with a small group or prayer partnership, not finding ways to use their gifts to serve at church, or having some secret and unaddressed sin.

▶ **WATCH DVD 7.1** (7 min 59 sec) **OR DELIVER TALK 7.1** (see page 144)

* *Encourage the group to make notes as they watch the DVD or listen to the talk. There is space for notes on page 135 of the Handbook.*

Discuss

ROMANS 12:9-13

⁹ Let love be genuine. Abhor what is evil; hold fast to what is good. ¹⁰ Love one another with brotherly affection. Outdo one another in showing honor. ¹¹ Do not be slothful in zeal, be fervent in spirit, serve the Lord. ¹² Rejoice in hope, be patient in tribulation, be constant in prayer. ¹³ Contribute to the needs of the saints and seek to show hospitality.

"Let love be genuine." What is the difference between being "nice" or "tolerant," and genuine Christian love?

"It's nice to be nice"—but it isn't always loving! Paul tells us to "abhor what is evil," whereas "tolerance" accepts all but the most extreme sinful behavior. Christian love won't pretend that something is good when it isn't, or keep quiet when someone is involved in sinful behavior. However, Christian love is also much greater and deeper than mere "niceness"—a Christian who is reflecting the love shown to them by God will be willing to put someone else's preferences before their own, forgive those who sin against them, and serve others sacrificially.

Why is this love only possible through the gospel?

We are reflecting the undeserved love and forgiveness shown to us by God. This doesn't come to us naturally, so we need consciously to reflect on the gospel and ask the Spirit to work in our hearts in order to overcome our selfishness and show genuine love.

What might it look like for us to "outdo one another in showing honor"?

Verse 10 refers to "one another" twice: we are to "love one another with brotherly affection" and also to "outdo one another in showing honor." So, as we love each other, we will want to encourage and honor each other's gifts and good deeds. We won't be jealous when someone is good at something, but instead will want to rejoice in what they are able to do. And when we talk about each other, it won't be spiteful gossip, but an opportunity to point to the gifts God has given someone, and rejoice in how he is working in their life. We will point to others and honor them, rather than seeking to point to ourselves so that others will honor us.

What kind of reputation does your church have in your community? How could a church's reputation—and the reputation of Jesus—be compromised by the lack of love of individual members?

Think about the people living near to the building where you hold your worship services:
- What reputation will the church have with them? This may be linked with the

location (eg: Do all the local roads get parked up with church members?

- Do you have a church lawn you open for local residents to enjoy sitting on?), or with what you do as a church (eg: Do you offer a food bank for families who are struggling financially?
- Do you complain in a way that invites confrontation when someone parks on church property?
- Are your services explicitly welcoming, or unconcsiously unwelcoming?).

NOTE: Having a "bad" reputation isn't necessarily a bad thing. For example, the church in Thessalonica (Acts 17:4-9) had such a "bad reputation" with the local people that these people started a riot. But if we do have a "bad" reputation, it must be because we are being shaped by the gospel and seeking to share the gospel, not because we are being unloving and inconsiderate neighbors.

▶ **WATCH DVD 7.2** (5 min 43 sec) **OR DELIVER TALK 7.2** (see page 144)

- *Encourage the group to make notes as they watch the DVD or listen to the talk. There is space for notes on page 137 of the Handbook.*

Discuss

👉 **ROMANS 12:14-18**

[14] Bless those who persecute you; bless and do not curse them. [15] Rejoice with those who rejoice, weep with those who weep. [16] Live in harmony with one another. Do not be haughty, but associate with the lowly. Never be wise in your own sight. [17] Repay no one evil for evil, but give thought to do what is honorable in the sight of all. [18] If possible, so far as it depends on you, live peaceably with all.

In what ways is "being church" different from "going to church"?

"Going to church" is about attending the worship services and maybe a midweek group. "Being church" is about being family together, loving one another and encouraging each other as followers of Jesus. It demands that we are open with our lives and our homes, and commit our time to one another, even (or especially) when that is sacrificial.

"We come up with all kinds of reasons and excuses to keep our distance from each other." **What are some of them? How does the gospel address these reasons and push Christians closer together?**

Possible "reasons and excuses" might be:
- **Family:** We spend most of our time with our own family.
- **Busyness:** We allow our lives to be so busy that we have no time to spend with our church family other than at formal worship services, or maybe a midweek group.
- **Hiding our real lives:** We "wear our Sunday best," telling everyone that we are fine, rather than being open about our real lives, struggles, etc.
- **Putting up barriers:** We don't allow ourselves to be challenged or encouraged by others.

The gospel pushes us together because:
- **Family:** The gospel puts us in a new family. We have responsibilities to our human family, but we also have a responsibility to our new spiritual family.
- **Busyness:** The gospel gives us new priorities around serving Christ in all our lives. This will inevitably change what we find important. We may need to challenge each other over what we are "busy" about.
- **Hiding our real lives:** The gospel tells us that we have no ability or need to hide from God, and therefore we can be real about ourselves with other Christians.
- **Putting up barriers:** The gospel shows us what true love is and challenges us to reflect that in our own lives. The gospel corrects our selfish tendency to be "me-centered" and undermines our idols.

▶ **WATCH DVD 7.3** (4 min 51 sec) **OR DELIVER TALK 7.3** (see page 144)

- *Encourage the group to make notes as they watch the DVD or listen to the talk. There is space for notes on page 138 of the Handbook.*

Discuss

We started this series by asking what comes into your mind when you hear the word "worship." How would you answer that now?

Ask group members to write their answer in their Handbooks, using their own words. Do this first before asking some of them to share their answers.

What new aspect(s) of worship has/have come into focus for you over the past weeks?

If people struggle to think of anything, suggest that they look through the contents list on page 5 of the Handbook. This will remind them about the different topics they've looked at during the course.

Look back over your notes and journal for the previous weeks. How will the gospel make a practical difference to your own worship:
- **as a member of your church?**
- **in your home?**
- **as part of your community?**

Most of these studies ended with deciding on some practical ways to respond to each session's teaching. Encourage people to look up what they wrote at the time, as well as anything they may have written in the weekly journal. If you have time, ask how the group have been getting on with living out some of the action points they have from earlier in the course.

Pray

Pray that your love for one another, and for your neighborhood, will be genuine.

Look at the practical things you have written at the top of this page. Pray that you will be able to put these into practice.

DAILY BIBLE DEVOTIONALS

The final set of devotionals works through Ephesians 4:1 – 6:9, where Paul lays out for believers how to live a life worthy of the calling they have been received— that is, how to respond to the great gospel truths of the first half of the letter by praising and worshiping God with their lives. Paul shows us how we can worship as church, in our personal holiness, at home and at work. Do encourage your group to use this last week of studies, even if they have not done the previous ones.

SERMONS

OPTION ONE: ROMANS 12:1-21

Jared focuses on Romans 12:9-21 in his DVD presentation, and it is also the subject of the Bible study (see next page), along with verses 1-2; but there is so much to study and enjoy in this passage that you could also expand upon it in a longer sermon.

OPTION TWO: 1 CORINTHIANS 13:1-13

This passage is not mentioned in this material, but helps us focus on the basis for all we are and do as church—Christ-like love:
- Love is fundamental (v 1-3): without it, all we are or do is "nothing."
- Love is Christ-like (v 4-7): he embodies the love described here.
- Love is eternal (v 8-13): we will one day enjoy God's love face to face, and love perfectly ourselves.

If one of your Sunday sermons is to be based on the theme of this session, church members will find a page to write notes on the sermon on page 151 of their Handbooks.

BIBLE STUDY

AIM: In this last session we put together many of the themes we have been looking at over the last seven weeks; in particular, emphasizing how true worship is much more than simply "going to church" or attending formal church meetings. We worship Jesus as we live grace-filled lives that are on show to outsiders through our day-to-day interactions as the church family—and as we show practical compassion to the world.

Discuss

In the old Anglican marriage service, the groom promises: "With my body, I thee worship." What would that kind of "worship" look like in a marriage?

☞ READ ROMANS 12:1-2; 9-21

> *¹ I appeal to you therefore, brothers, by the mercies of God, to present your bodies as a living sacrifice, holy and acceptable to God, which is your spiritual worship.*

Paul has explained the blessings of the gospel in great detail in chapters 1 – 11. He now comes to talk about the implications of this for how we live.

1. In verse 1 how does Paul define what true worship is?

It is presenting our bodies to God as a living sacrifice.

What reasons are we given why we should do this?

- "By the mercies of God" (v 1). Because of what God has done for us in the gospel. (Note: The NIV makes this clearer: "In view of God's mercy").
- "Holy and acceptable to God" (v 2). This is the worship that God wants from us; ie: not just church attendance, or the sacrifice of anything less than our whole selves. It pleases God, and enables us to live lives that are set apart for him.

151

2. **Paul does not start his description of our response to the gospel with a list of commands. How is what he says in v 1-2 different from what people assume drives Christian living?**

- *It is about worshiping the God who saved us*; it's not primarily about obedience to rules out of guilt. The gospel says we are free from guilt and sin through the cross of Christ. The gospel now calls us to live in light of that.
- *It's about our bodies.* Many people assume being religious is a "spiritual thing" just to do with our spirit—feelings, emotions, etc. The gospel says it is about what we do with our bodies.
- *It's about our minds.* Non-Christians caricature Christian belief as "mindless"— *Don't think; just have faith.* The gospel says: *Do think*, but we do this with the mind of God.

3. **Look over the encouragements in v 9-13. Describe what a Christian life based on these verses would look like. How would "Chris" or "Christina" spend their spare time? How would they react to problems in their lives? How would they react to problems in the lives of others?**

Get the group to talk out the practical meaning of these verses using this creative idea.

Describe a Christian you know who you think exemplifies one of these characteristics.

Again, the aim is to see what this list looks like in real life, and get the group to "feel" how admirable these Christ-like qualities are in others. Don't embarrass anyone in the group if they are named during this discussion.

4. **Which of the instructions in v 14, 15 and 16 do you find hardest to obey, and why? How could you help each other to grow these qualities in your lives?**

- Be listening for particular problems people may have with being bullied or persecuted by colleagues, friends and family—or struggles in other areas of their Christian lives.
- We need to keep reminding each other of the gospel basis for why we live as we do.
- We need to encourage each other to keep going—sharing our own struggles and joys.

5. Why is the instruction in v 17 and 19 especially difficult for us to follow?

We find it hard to not take revenge because we have a proper sense of justice, but one that is often warped by our tendency to interpret selfishly the harm caused to us. When we take revenge, we tend to escalate the problem, not end it.

What encouragement does Paul give to help us do this?

Paul says that God will judge—he will do it far more effectively, wisely and appropriately than we ever could.

6. What must we do instead (v 20)? How does this show the gospel to unbelievers?

We are to love them, and show kindness. In doing so we will "heap burning coals on [their] head." This most likely means that they will be shamed by their sin, and come to repentance over it—in other words, our love and kindness is one way in which God can lead people to the gospel of grace, through our obedience to it.

In the gospel, God did not judge and punish us, but his own Son instead. To live a life marked by love, forgiveness and grace shows others the love and grace of God, who has forgiven us.

7. Look back over your prayer requests and personal applications from previous weeks, and review your personal journal. What has the Lord taught you that is to you new over the last seven weeks? What has been reinforced in your thinking about the Christian life?

How will this make you think differently about:
- **your own personal holiness and growth as a follower of Christ?**
- **the way you think about gathering with other believers?**
- **your outreach to friends and family?**

Depending on the make-up of your group, you may decide to allow them time to fill these things in privately, or share them with the group.

Apply

FOR YOURSELF: Which of the areas of obedience listed in the passage do you think you are doing well in? Where might you need some more encouragement?

FOR YOUR CHURCH: Which of the areas of obedience listed in the passage do you think your church does well in? Where could it use a little more help and stimulation?

Pray

Pray that you would grow as a true worshiper of God; and that the worship of your church would be acceptable to him.

FURTHER READING

Jesus did not save you to be a lone ranger; he saved you to live as a church member and enjoy eternity in his city, living with others.
Mike McKinley

How we do church reflects how much we value Jesus. The more we see how wonderful he is, the more we will love being part of his church, a small stone in the great grandeur of God's cosmic, eternal building.
Ray Ortlund

Books

- *The Deliberate Church (Mark Dever & Paul Alexander)*
- *Gospel-Centered Church (Steve Timmis & Tim Chester)*
- *Evangelism: How the Whole Church Speaks of Jesus (Mack Stiles)*
- *Jesus-Driven Ministry (Ajith Fernando)*
- *What is a Healthy Church Member? (Thabiti Anyabwile)*
- *The Prodigal Church (Jared Wilson)*

Online

- *How to get a Real Honest Community*
  gospelshapedchurch.org/resources171
- *Saved by a Community, For a Community*
  gospelshapedchurch.org/resources172
- *The Insufficiency of Small Groups for Discipleship*
  gospelshapedchurch.org/resources173

LEADER'S REFLECTIONS

GOSPEL SHAPED

CHURCH

The complete series

LET THE POWER OF THE GOSPEL SHAPE FOUR OTHER CRITICAL AREAS IN THE LIFE OF YOUR CHURCH

GOSPEL SHAPED
OUTREACH

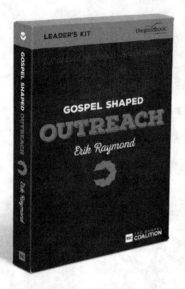

Many Christians are nervous about telling someone else about Jesus. The nine sessions in this curriculum don't offer quick fixes or evangelism "gimmicks." But by continually pointing us back to the gospel, they will give us the proper motivation to work together as a church to share the gospel message with those who are lost without Christ.

As you work through the material, you will discover that God's mission of salvation in the world is also your mission; and that he is inviting you into the privilege of praying and working to advance his kingdom among your family, friends, neighbors, co-workers and community.

Gospel Shaped Church is a new curriculum from The Gospel Coalition that will help whole congregations pause and think slowly, carefully and prayerfully about the kind of church they are called to be.

Written and presented by **ERIK RAYMOND**
Erik is the Preaching Pastor at Emmaus Bible Church in Omaha, Nebraska. He is married to Christie and has six children.

WWW.GOSPELSHAPEDCHURCH.ORG/OUTREACH

"WE WANT CHURCHES CALLED INTO EXISTENCE BY THE GOSPEL TO BE SHAPED BY THE GOSPEL IN THEIR EVERYDAY LIFE."

DON CARSON AND TIM KELLER

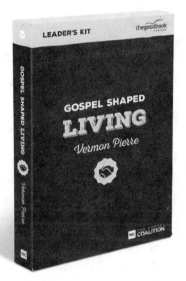

GOSPEL SHAPED
LIVING

Gospel Shaped Living is a track that explores over seven sessions what it means for a local church to be a distinctive counter-cultural community.

Through the gospel, God calls people from every nation, race and background to be joined together in a new family that shows his grace and glory. How should our lives as individuals and as a church reflect and model the new life we have found in Christ? And how different should we be to the world around us?

This challenging and interactive course will inspire us to celebrate grace and let the gospel shape our lives day by day.

Written and presented by **VERMON PIERRE**
Vermon is the Lead Pastor of Roosevelt Community Church in Phoenix, Arizona. He is married to Dennae and has three children. photo: Bradford Armstrong

WWW.GOSPELSHAPEDCHURCH.ORG/LIVING

GOSPEL SHAPED
WORK

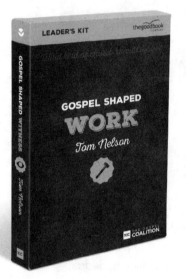

Many Christians experience a troubling disconnect between their everyday work and what they live and work for as a believer in Jesus. How should the gospel shape my view of life on an assembly line, or change my work as a teacher, artist, nurse, home-maker or gardener?

Gospel Shaped Work explores over eight sessions how the gospel changes the way we view our work in the world—and how a church should equip its members to serve God in their everyday vocations, and relate to the wider world of work and culture.

These engaging and practical sessions are designed to reveal the Bible's all-encompassing vision for our daily lives, and our engagement with culture as a redeemed community. It will provoke a fresh discussion in your church about how the gospel of Christ impacts every area of life in our world.

Written and presented by **TOM NELSON**
Tom is the Senior Pastor of Christ Community Church in Kansas City, and a council member of The Gospel Coalition. He is married to Liz and has two grown children.

WWW.GOSPELSHAPEDCHURCH.ORG/WORK

"THESE RESOURCES GIVE SPACE TO CONSIDER WHAT A GENUINE EXPRESSION OF A GOSPEL-SHAPED CHURCH LOOKS LIKE FOR YOU IN THE PLACE GOD HAS PUT YOU, AND WITH THE PEOPLE HE HAS GATHERED INTO FELLOWSHIP WITH YOU."

DON CARSON AND TIM KELLER

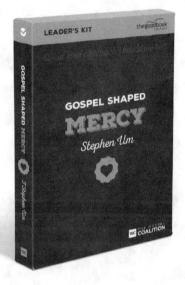

GOSPEL SHAPED
MERCY

The gospel is all about justice and mercy: the just punishment of God falling on his Son, Jesus, so that he can have mercy on me, a sinner.

But many churches have avoided following through on the Bible's clear teaching on working for justice and mercy in the wider world. They fear that it is a distraction from the primary task of gospel preaching.

This *Gospel Shaped Mercy* module explores how individual Christians and whole churches can and should be engaged in the relief of poverty, hunger and injustice in a way that adorns the gospel of grace.

Written and presented by **STEPHEN UM**
Stephen is Senior Minister of Citylife Church in Boston, MA, and is a council member of The Gospel Coalition.

WWW.GOSPELSHAPEDCHURCH.ORG/MERCY

MORE RESOURCES
TO HELP SHAPE YOUR
WORSHIP

Let **the gospel** frame the way you **think and feel**

This workbook shows how ordinary Christians can live the life that God calls us to. By focusing our attention on the gospel, everyday problems familiar to Christians everywhere can be transformed as the cross of Christ becomes the motive and measure of everything we do. *Gospel Centered Life* shows how every Christian can follow the way of the cross as they embrace the liberating grace of God in Christ.

STEVE TIMMIS is Global Director for Acts 29

TIM CHESTER is Director of the Porterbrook Seminary

WWW.THEGOODBOOK.COM/GCL

LIVEDIFFERENT

> " I HAVE COME THAT THEY MAY HAVE
> LIFE AND HAVE IT TO THE FULL. "
> —— JOHN 10:10 ——

"As I was reading John's book, I found myself in conversations with some of the very people it addresses – people who serve, but who are growing weary of serving. It was a joy to recommend the book to them."

Tim Challies
BLOGGER & AUTHOR

This warm and pastoral book by Tim Lane helps readers to see when godly concern turns into sinful worry, and how Scripture can be used to cast those worries upon the Lord. You will discover how to replace anxiety with peace in your life, freeing you to live life to the full.

TIM LANE is President of the Institute for Pastoral Care, USA, and author of *How People Change*

WWW.THEGOODBOOK.COM/LD

LIVE | GROW | KNOW

Live with Christ, Grow in Christ, Know more of Christ.

"These studies by Becky Pippert are clear and accessible, yet substantial and thoughtful explorations of how to be grounded and grow in Christian faith. They evidence years of experience working with people at all stages of belief and skepticism. I highly recommend them."

Tim Keller

PART 1

live

Explores what the Christian life is like.

Ever got to the end of running an evangelistic course and wondered: What next?

LiveGrowKnow is a brand-new series from globally renowned speaker Rebecca Manley Pippert, designed to help people continue their journey from enquirer to disciple to mature believer.

Part 1, Live, consists of five DVD-based sessions and is the perfect follow-up to an evangelistic course or event, or for anyone who wants to explore the Christian life more deeply.

REBECCA MANLEY PIPPERT
Globally-renowned speaker and author of
Out of the Saltshaker

PART **2**

grow

Explores how we
mature as Christians.

I'm a Christian… what next?
These studies show what God's plan for
our lives is, and how we can get going
and get growing in the Christian life.
For groups who have done the LIVE
course, GROW is the follow-up; it also
works perfectly as a stand-alone course
for groups wishing to think about how
to grow in a real, and exciting, way.
Handbook and DVD available.

PART **3**

know

Looks at core
doctrines of the faith.

the good**book**
COMPANY

thegoodbook
COMPANY
Opening up the Bible

At The Good Book Company, we are dedicated to helping Christians and local churches grow. We believe that God's growth process always starts with hearing clearly what he has said to us through his timeless word—the Bible.

Ever since we opened our doors in 1991, we have been striving to produce resources that honor God in the way the Bible is used. We have grown to become an international provider of user-friendly resources to the Christian community, with believers of all backgrounds and denominations using our Bible studies, books, evangelistic resources, DVD-based courses and training events.

We want to equip ordinary Christians to live for Christ day by day, and churches to grow in their knowledge of God, their love for one another, and the effectiveness of their outreach.

Call us for a discussion of your needs or visit one of our local websites for more information on the resources and services we provide.

North America: www.thegoodbook.com
UK & Europe: www.thegoodbook.co.uk
Australia: www.thegoodbook.com.au
New Zealand: www.thegoodbook.co.nz

North America: 866 244 2165
UK & Europe: 0333 123 0880
Australia: (02) 6100 4211
New Zealand (+64) 3 343 1990